BANISHED
A GRANDMOTHER ALONE

*Surviving Alienation
and
Estrangement*

NANCY LEE KLUNE

BALBOA.
PRESS
A DIVISION OF HAY HOUSE

Copyright © 2018 Nancy Lee Klune.

All rights reserved. No part of this book may be used or reproduced by any means, graphic, electronic, or mechanical, including photocopying, recording, taping or by any information storage retrieval system without the written permission of the author except in the case of brief quotations embodied in critical articles and reviews.

This book is a work of non-fiction. Unless otherwise noted, the author and the publisher make no explicit guarantees as to the accuracy of the information contained in this book and in some cases, names of people and places have been altered to protect their privacy.

Balboa Press books may be ordered through booksellers or by contacting:

Balboa Press
A Division of Hay House
1663 Liberty Drive
Bloomington, IN 47403
www.balboapress.com
1 (877) 407-4847

Because of the dynamic nature of the Internet, any web addresses or links contained in this book may have changed since publication and may no longer be valid. The views expressed in this work are solely those of the author and do not necessarily reflect the views of the publisher, and the publisher hereby disclaims any responsibility for them.

The author of this book does not dispense medical advice or prescribe the use of any technique as a form of treatment for physical, emotional, or medical problems without the advice of a physician, either directly or indirectly. The intent of the author is only to offer information of a general nature to help you in your quest for emotional and spiritual well-being. In the event you use any of the information in this book for yourself, which is your constitutional right, the author and the publisher assume no responsibility for your actions.

Any people depicted in stock imagery provided by Getty Images are models, and such images are being used for illustrative purposes only.
Certain stock imagery © Getty Images.

Print information available on the last page.

ISBN: 978-1-9822-1386-2 (sc)
ISBN: 978-1-9822-1388-6 (hc)
ISBN: 978-1-9822-1387-9 (e)

Library of Congress Control Number: 2018912003

Balboa Press rev. date: 12/06/2018

To my grandchildren:
I carry you in my heart.

How to Use This Book

Read this book from cover to cover, one chapter at a time, or choose a subject you feel drawn to on any given day. Certain ideas and strategies are revisited throughout in order to emphasize their importance. Open the book randomly for guidance, or use it as a reference for healing, insight, and comfort.

Contents

Introduction xiii
1. Starting Where You Are 1
2. Grief 3
3. Loneliness 5
4. Loving Yourself 7
5. It Will Get Better 9
6. Getting Your Mojo Back 11
7. Emotional Triggers 13
8. Optimism 16
9. Who Are You Now? 18
10. In-Laws 20
11. Don't Take It Personally 22
12. Powerlessness 24
13. Stranger in a Strange Land 26
14. Missing Your Adult Child 28
15. Letting Go 31
16. Depression 34
17. Shame 37
18. What Does Your Soul Need? 39
19. Older and Wiser 41
20. Birthdays 43
21. Humor 45
22. Compassion 47
23. Acceptance 49

24.	Appreciation	51
25.	Self-Talk	53
26.	HALT	55
27.	Dark Night of the Soul	57
28.	Getting Help	59
29.	Managing Anger	61
30.	Ups and Downs	63
31.	Self-Soothing	65
32.	Mindful Moments	67
33.	Surrendering	69
34.	Stuck in the Victim Role	71
35.	Being Happy Anyway	74
36.	The Present	76
37.	Turnaround Thoughts	78
38.	Keeping It Simple	80
39.	Music	82
40.	Healthy Self-Respect	84
41.	Mother's Day	86
42.	Nourishing Your Mind	88
43.	The Importance of Play	90
44.	Managing Moods	92
45.	Thanksgiving	94
46.	Morning and Evening Rituals	96
47.	Giving Back	98
48.	Perceptions	100
49.	Everything Changes	102
50.	Backsliding	104
51.	Forgiving Yourself	106
52.	Walking	108
53.	The Problem with Comparisons	110
54.	Codependency	113
55.	Detachment	115
56.	Making Amends	117

57.	Coulda, Shoulda, Woulda	119
58.	Tough Love	121
59.	The Worry Habit	123
60.	Detoxing	125
61.	Healthy Relationships	128
62.	Believing You're Good Enough	130
63.	Higher Ground	132
64.	Planning Ahead	134
65.	Choices	136
66.	Christmas	138
67.	Integrity	140
68.	Taking Care of Yourself	142
69.	Solitude	144
70.	Changing Your Story	146
71.	The Beauty around You	150
72.	Self-Validation	151
73.	Comfort in Small Miracles	153
74.	When to Walk Away	155
75.	Finding Solace	157
76.	Building Character and Strength	159
77.	Collateral Damage	161
78.	Transcending Pain	163
79.	Creating a Vision for Your Life	166
80.	Your Home, Your Sanctuary	168
81.	Slaying the Dragons within You	170
82.	As Time Goes By	172
83.	And Still You Rise	174
84.	Blessing Others	176
85.	Gratitude	178
86.	No Stone Left Unturned	180
87.	Being the Hero of Your Story	182
88.	Keeping It Real	184
89.	Forgiveness	186

90. Practice, Practice, Practice 188
91. Honoring Yourself 191
92. Keeping Hope Alive.. 193
93. Carrying On.. 195
94. Loving Them Anyway 198

Epilogue... 201
About the Author 203

Introduction

Years ago, I received a phone call from a man who introduced himself as a family therapist who was working with my son and his wife. When I asked why he was calling *me*, he replied that my son and daughter-in-law had asked him to inform me that they wanted me out of their lives. He said they felt their marriage was happier without my drama. From that day forward, I was cut out of the lives of my four grandchildren. I was given no explanation or reason, only that my son and daughter-in-law had decided to send me packing.

I was stunned, to say the least.

However, this book is not about the story. The reasons for the estrangement exist in the minds of those who chose to excommunicate me. I am not interested in shaming, blaming, or defaming anyone. I can't argue their perceptions, and I have no say in their decision to ostracize me from my loved ones.

In living through the heartbreak of estrangement, I discovered that I'm not alone. There are thousands, perhaps hundreds of thousands, of parents and grandparents who have been similarly shunned by their families. As I began to heal from my own tribulations, it occurred to me that by sharing what I've learned, I might help others who are also experiencing alienation and estrangement.

Within these pages, I share my process of healing. I talk about acceptance, forgiveness, gratitude, self-love, and the importance of letting go and honoring your own life. I reveal how I've found joy and happiness again, despite the vacuum created by the absence of my adult child and grandchildren.

I'm no different from you: I'm a parent who loves her family, including her estranged child and grandchildren. Being cast out from them broke my heart, but broken hearts can mend. It takes time, effort, patience, and loving kindness toward ourselves, but it can be done.

I write as a fellow traveler who was brought to my knees by alienation and estrangement. If you, too, are a grandparent who has been denied access to your grandchildren or a hurting parent who has been rejected by your adult child, my wish is that this book will help you move forward, while offering tools for healing and creating more love and peace in your life.

Most of all, I hope you will find comfort in the knowledge that you're not alone.

Butterfly Laughter

In the middle of our porridge plates
There was a blue butterfly painted
And each morning we tried who should reach the
butterfly first.
Then the Grandmother said: "Do not eat the poor
butterfly."
That made us laugh.
Always she said it and always it started us laughing.
It seemed such a sweet little joke.
I was certain that one fine morning
The butterfly would fly out of our plates,
Laughing the teeniest laugh in the world,
And perch on the Grandmother's lap.
—Katherine Mansfield

1. Starting Where You Are

If you've recently been estranged or alienated from members of your family, please be gentle with yourself. You may be in shock and experiencing enormous stress, pain, and trauma. Treat yourself with loving compassion, even if it seems like the last thing you feel able to do. Just start where you are and be aware that you need time to assimilate and process what has happened.

The reasons for your estrangement may be unclear to you. Perhaps you have been scapegoated by your adult child's partner or spouse, or accused of misdeeds by a gatekeeper. Maybe your child's judgment has been clouded by anger, confusion, or addiction. Whatever the reasons, it's possible that you feel like you've been sentenced to a life in exile.

Fear may be assaulting you day and night. You fear this is the end of a dream, that you'll miss out on knowing your grandchildren. You experience overwhelming anxiety, compounded by guilt and shame. You may feel like you can't go on, that life is no longer worth living. Although you did everything within your power to understand the problem your alienator has with you, deep down, you fear that you are somehow to blame for this awful abandonment.

It's okay to feel your sorrow. It's okay to feel lost. It's important to experience all your feelings—shock, fear, grief, rage, hurt, guilt, and shame—because these emotions are predictable responses to the stress of being incomprehensibly shaken loose from your family tree. Allow yourself to ride these waves of heartbreak because if you don't, they will engulf you.

Little by little, you will turn away from the pain. Of course, this takes time. Read books, blogs, and articles on the subjects of estrangement and alienation. Find a therapist or life coach; a trusted priest, minister, or rabbi; or a support group for alienated parents and grandparents. Then slowly start doing the work necessary to begin again. If you have religious or spiritual beliefs, this would be a good time to delve into and practice the tenets of your faith; if you meditate, continue to do so. If you're not in the habit of meditating or praying, you might consider exploring these practices.

But for now, take baby steps. For example, today, set aside a few minutes to sit quietly, take a few deep breaths, close your eyes, and calm your mind. Tomorrow, go outside and take a walk. If you've been isolating yourself at home, even going for a stroll around the block is progress. Saint Francis of Assisi said, "Start by doing what's necessary; then do what's possible; and suddenly you are doing the impossible." Each day, introduce something new, like doing morning stretches or planting spring flowers under the healing warmth of the sun.

By learning to choose thoughts and activities that comfort and support, you will get through this. You will come to understand that you have little or no control over the circumstances of this estrangement. This knowledge and insight will ultimately propel you toward greater acceptance, strength, and wisdom as you find your way back home to yourself.

> What saves a man is to take a step. Then another step.
> —Antoine de Saint-Exupery

2. Grief

> Should you shield the canyons from the windstorms,
> you would never see the beauty of their carvings.
> —Elizabeth Kubler-Ross

There are days when you feel like you're drowning in grief. You cry until you can't breathe. You feel helpless and betrayed. You keep asking yourself how this happened, what you did wrong, and what you can do to facilitate reconciliation. You may have regrets, and your heart may be heavy. You may have fallen into the "if only" pit, in which you obsess about what you said or didn't say, or what you did or didn't do. But going over and over past events only exacerbates your grief and sadness.

Parents and grandparents who are estranged from their adult child and alienated from their grandchildren experience an ambiguous grief. Ambiguous because a loss of this kind leaves you feeling disenfranchised, searching for reasons, and seeking answers. Your grief is a natural reaction to being torn from those you love, but due to the lack of closure, the grieving process can seem endless. Being aware of this will help you better understand the ongoing nature of the distress, fear, and sadness you feel and can ultimately help mitigate your grief.

Writer C. S. Lewis said that grief feels like fear: a "fluttering in the stomach, the same restlessness, the yawning." Grief has many facets, one of which is fear. For example, you may fear that the situation won't resolve, that you'll miss out on knowing your grandchildren or that the grief you're feeling will consume you.

In the words of philosopher Friedrich Nietzsche, "To live is to suffer, to survive is to find some meaning in the suffering." Know that one day, your grief will abate and your cycles of despair, anger, and sadness will grow less debilitating. You will experience a purification, a cleansing. You will undergo an inner spiritual growth spurt. You may never completely heal from the trauma of banishment and estrangement, but if you choose to do the work necessary for your personal transformation, you will grow in wisdom and find meaning in your life.

It is courageous to feel the depths of your grief. By embracing the tough reality of your loss, mourning it, assimilating it, and feeling your sorrow and hurt, you will eventually create a space in your heart for acceptance of what is and a deep sense of peace.

> When our days become dreary with low-hovering clouds of despair, and when our nights become darker than a thousand midnights, let us remember that there is a creative force in this universe, working to pull down the gigantic mountains of evil, a power that is able to make a way out of no way and transform dark yesterdays into bright tomorrows. Let us realize the arc of the moral universe is long but it bends toward justice.
> —Martin Luther King Jr.

3. Loneliness

> It is good to be lonely, for being alone is not easy. The fact that something is difficult must be one more reason to do it.
>
> —Rilke

In the wake of being alienated and abandoned, the loneliness is so profound that it can feel like you're falling into a black hole. One day, you wake up with no bearings, stumbling into uncharted territory.

At some point during the aftermath of alienation, you will feel the need to grieve. It's healthy to feel your anguish, so let yourself fully experience this passage. This is the beginning of healing and recovery from the trauma.

There were times, especially in the early stages of estrangement, when I felt so lonely, I didn't know how I'd make it through another day. I was haunted by mistakes I'd made in the past when I was a clueless young mother, mindlessly teaching what I had learned as a child from my own parents, who were then young and damaged themselves. I was terrified of a future alone, without the companionship and love of my family. I still have days when I feel overwhelmed with sadness, but I have learned to reach out and talk to someone who understands, like a close friend or therapist. It can be scary to feel lost and alone, but if you're willing, it can be a time of learning more about yourself—who you've been and who you are now. You can decide to make the changes necessary to become the person you want to be. Persian poet Hafiz wrote, "Don't surrender your loneliness so quickly. Let it cut you more deep. Let it ferment and season you as few humans and even divine ingredients can."

Loneliness is challenging, but it can be a positive passage if you choose to make good use of it. No one can fill the vacuum created by your grandchildren's absence, but if you work at it, you can fill this emptiness with love—for yourself, for others, and for the ultimate goodness of life.

> Loneliness accepted becomes a gift leading one from a life dominated by tears to the discovery of one's true self and finally to the heart of longing and the love of God.
> —Unknown

4. Loving Yourself

We have been conditioned throughout our lives to believe that our happiness is dependent upon how others perceive us and treat us. Since childhood, we have been invested in gaining approval and acting in ways that give us what we want, which is love.

We inherently loved ourselves as small children. We were in love with life and with exploring what our little bodies were capable of, like joyously doing somersaults, turning cartwheels, or riding a bicycle. At first, we were just in the moment, loving what we were doing and enjoying our discoveries. Too soon, however, our focus shifted from our cartwheels and handstands to others' responses to us, and that was when our happiness became dependent on their approbation and love. As a result, the locus of control moved from inside to outside of ourselves, which compromised our instinct for self-love.

Because you have experienced problems with your adult child, you may be faltering in your ability to love yourself. You wonder if there is something wrong with you because your own child has disapproved of you and is withholding love. Nothing is gained by taking this view. Other people's behaviors, even your grown children, come from their own perceptions and may have nothing to do with reality. As difficult as it may be to accept, you don't need their approval (or even their love) to live a happy and fulfilling life.

"When you look deep inside yourself, you will find that love is always there ... for yourself and everyone else," writes Don Miguel

Ruiz Jr. Fall in love with yourself again. Rediscover that precious child within you who was overjoyed to run, hop, skip, and jump just for the fun of it. Fall in love with your life, your home, and your family and friends. Love everyday occurrences, like the smell of clean laundry and the gift of running water. Love who you are and who you aren't. Love your body, your mind, and your unique, authentic self. Love your quirks, imperfections, and foibles. Love your talents and the maturity and wisdom you've acquired. Love your beautiful spirit, for in loving yourself, your heart will overflow with love for everyone.

> Accept yourself. Love yourself as you are. Your finest work, your best movements, your joy, peace, and healing comes when you love yourself. You give a great gift to the world when you do that. You give others permission to do the same: to love themselves. Revel in self-love. Roll in it. Bask in it as you would sunshine.
> —Melodie Beattie

5. It Will Get Better

When alienation happens, we parents and grandparents are unable to make sense of it, and we feel like we're suspended in a timeless agony.

It seems like the pain will last forever, but it doesn't.

Time passes. Days continue to dawn, and the sun continues to set. At some point, however, we notice a new rhythm to our days; our breath flows more freely, our eyes are clearer, and we smile more readily. Food tastes better; colors are brighter.

As heartbreaking as it is for me still, I have learned that even without the desired reconciliation and healing from estrangement, the pain does abate. Over time, the cycles of crippling despair become shorter and less intense. I believe there is a law of compensation at work that offers reparation for our losses. Psychologist William James said, "Believe that life is worth living, and your belief will help create the fact." For example, after allowing myself enough time to grieve and to assimilate the reality of being estranged from my son and his wife, I deliberately chose to embrace life again. As a result, I have had experiences I never would have had, such as hiking on distant mountains, making wonderful new friends, living in the woods, and starting to write. These adventures stretched, challenged, and transformed me and enriched my life in miraculous ways.

As we grow older, life becomes extremely precious, and we become acutely aware that our days are numbered. Because we have been through our darkest trials, we are thankful for the dawning of each new day, and we're eager for new experiences. We grow in wisdom and want to be of service to others. We become experts on letting go and loving unconditionally. We are kinder, gentler, and more in touch with the sanctity of our lives. And because we have been through so much, we have compassion for others who are facing unimaginable challenges.

> The best is yet to be.
> —Robert Browning

6. Getting Your Mojo Back

What is mojo? It is energy, vitality, zest for life, spirit, zip, zing, or passion. It's what makes us happy, keeps us empowered, and puts a bounce in our step.

Have you lost this wonderful feeling due to grieving or depression? If so, you can get your mojo working again, if you're willing. It's still there, nudging you to get your attention. Your creativity is yearning to be expressed, your voice is waiting to be heard, your laughter is bubbling up, ready to spread happiness.

Think about what hobbies and pursuits you may have neglected that you might revisit. Are you an artist who stopped painting? A gourmet cook who has started microwaving entire meals, a singer who stopped singing, or a gardener whose once flourishing garden is now choked with weeds? Ralph Waldo Emerson said, "All life is an experiment. The more experiments you make, the better." So get involved in activities that allow you to rediscover a part of you that you've left untended. It may be time to stretch yourself and move out of your comfort zone.

Eventually, the bad days come around less often. Because I have practiced being proactive by staying healthy and finding a new spirituality, I am getting stronger. I am tapping into my interests and talents, with the intention of expanding, growing, and recapturing a sense of wonder.

Know that your sadness and all the feelings that go along with being cut out of your grandchildren's lives won't magically disappear.

But you can turn your attention away from that pain by focusing on your interests and all that's new and exciting.

> Hide not your talents. They for use were made.
> What's a sundial in the shade?
> —Benjamin Franklin

7. Emotional Triggers

How do you feel when your friends talk about their amazing, wonderful, adorable grandchildren? What do you do when they whip out their smartphones and start scrolling through pictures of them as they rhapsodize about how cute and smart they are?

You've reached a time in your life when many people you know are becoming grandparents, and it's inevitable that they'll bring up the subject of their grandchildren. Although it may be unreasonable to expect your friends to avoid the subject in deference to your estrangement, you might request that they limit how much time they talk about them. You might tell them that although you enjoy hearing about the kids and seeing their pictures, it's difficult for you because it reminds you of what you're missing. A good friend of mine was telling me, in great detail, about a recent visit with her grandchildren. After listening to her for what seemed like hours, I asked her if she'd be willing to limit the stories of her grandchildren to no more than two or three at a time, because with each story, my sadness increased. She kindly agreed, and it was a win-win because she didn't feel that she had to withhold her joy, and I could relax and share in her happiness.

Many people, places, things, and circumstances can activate a painful memory or an emotional response. For example, looking at pictures of your grandchildren on Instagram or Facebook, walking by a park where you played hide-and-go-seek with them, or driving by the public library where you brought them to borrow books can be painful triggers. Knowing that your grandchildren are spending time with their other grandparents, and not you, can be tough. Seeing families together at restaurants, children sitting on their grandparents' laps, laughing and having fun can be enough to send you running from the place. Holidays are also challenging, as are trips to the mall, movies, or any public place where families gather.

Author John G. Miller says, "Whatever the 'trigger event,' we always choose our own response. We choose to react angrily. We choose to stuff our emotions and keep quiet. We choose to worry." Being able to recognize and manage triggers is important, and having various coping mechanisms in place is vital for your own emotional survival. For instance, if you are in a situation where there are intact families, take a deep breath and, rather than falling into the abyss of feeling deprived of your grandchildren, switch your thoughts to the present moment. Scan your body and feel where the hurt is and gently breathe into it. For instance, I often feel a heaviness in my solar plexus when I'm sad, and I when I breathe into it, I am able to calm myself.

If your best efforts couldn't bring about a change in the abandonment and estrangement you are enduring, remember that things can always change for the better. For now, choose to create a meaningful life in spite of your circumstances. When necessary, compartmentalize, put your sorrows aside and enjoy the activities around you. I'm reminded of a little boy in my neighborhood who often waits for me in the early evenings when I walk my dog. We have a little visit, during which he tells me about whatever sports he's playing and about his day in general. He's someone else's grandson, true, but my relationship with him helps, in a small way, to fill up the vacuum left by my own grandchildren's absence.

Although, I am still not allowed to visit with my grandchildren, we now text from time to time. Recently, I received a text from my grandson telling me that he was on his way to visit his other grandparents and about all the fun things they were planning to do. This was a potentially deadly trigger for me, but I had a choice: I could get upset and envious, or I could make it about my grandson: his life, his emotional health, and his happiness. I chose the latter, and although I felt sad about being deprived of visits with him, I was happy that he texted me to share his excitement. I made it about him, not me, thereby avoiding a lethal trigger.

For an excommunicated parent and grandparent, the pain will abate over time, but there will always be a wounded part of you. Your life will never be the same, but it can be good and fulfilling, nonetheless. You will always be in "recovery," like an addict or alcoholic who must be vigilant in order to avoid any pitfalls that could precipitate relapse.

Be aware of triggers, like holidays spent without your family, or sudden reminders of your grandchildren, and have a plan for dealing with situations that are challenging. Treat yourself with loving kindness, because, in reality, you are recovering from a very serious condition called heartbreak.

> I've learned … that love, not time, heals all wounds.
> —Andy Rooney

8. Optimism

The fictional character Pollyanna always found something to be glad about and looked for the silver lining in everything. Researchers are finding that through the practice of positive thinking, we become more resilient when faced with adversity. By challenging negative thoughts and training ourselves to search for a silver lining, even in the worst of circumstances, we change not only our mood but our brain chemistry for the better. For example, I often think about how much I miss my son. Then I remember how stressful it was communicating with him in the past, and I am relieved that I am no longer experiencing so much hurt, dismay, and frustration. I miss him, but I'm calmer and happier without the stress. Silver lining.

What if your future turns out to be wonderful? What if the best is yet to come? What if your estrangement has a happy ending? There is no downside to imagining it so and no upside to staying stuck in your sad story and ruminating about it. So why not view your situation through the proverbial rose-colored glasses? By doing so, you look for the gift in your challenges and put a positive spin on it all. You're not deluding yourself or denying reality; instead, you're choosing to see everything in a better light. A rosy outlook is good for you and will help create a healthier body and mind.

By generating life-affirming ways of thinking, you strengthen new neural pathways. Be happy *now* instead of waiting for someone or some future event to make you happy. Even though you may feel like you're trapped in the pit of hell right now, you can start creating a more positive worldview. Happiness is a choice, and being miserable is a choice.

I'm learning to discipline my mind and practice optimism, even under my current challenging circumstances. For example, most mornings when I wake up, I take a deep breath, stretch, and tell myself how grateful I am for this day. I give thanks for my health, for my friends and loved ones, and for my happy dog, who is thrilled to be going for a walk on this beautiful morning. I chase any fears away and choose to believe that all is well. It's a great way to start the day.

Pollyanna always looked on the bright side, and we can too. Doing so may not solve the problem of alienation and estrangement, but it will make it less pervasive in our minds. And by practicing optimism, we give ourselves a priceless gift.

Go ahead: put on those rose-colored glasses. They look good on you.

> There is abundant reason to believe that optimism—big, little, and in between—is useful to a person because positive expectations can be self-fulfilling.
> —Christopher Peterson

9. Who Are You Now?

You were born, grew up, and became a parent. The life you nurtured also grew up and brought forth another life, and you became a grandparent. Round and round goes the circle of life.

You were taught to honor your parents. You honored them as best you could, and you expected to be honored and respected when you became a parent. You believed that you would always be an integral part of your family, a family you were instrumental in creating.

What happened? Are you now stripped of your rightful place in your family? How do you cope with this deplorable revision?

You cope by going on, taking one breath at a time, putting one foot in front of the other. You choose not to let your adult child's behaviors and perspectives, or anyone else's, for that matter, define you. You consciously decide that your life is precious, and you treat it as such. You experience a sea change.

Yes, you grieve, and you're sure you'll die from the heartache. But you don't. You go on and expand your capacity for resilience, gratitude, and love. You grow in faith and take nothing for granted. Each day, each moment becomes a gift.

I was once an involved, dedicated, and loving grandmother. Since being cut out of the lives of my grandchildren, I have learned to live with a broken heart. However, if I perceived myself as a sad, lonely, aging woman with no grandchildren and no relationship with my adult child, I would feel sorry for myself every minute of every day. After so many years of dealing with estrangement, I refuse to be that person. I no longer accept that feeling sorry for myself is an option. I once enjoyed normal contact with my son and grandchildren, but that was another time. I am living a new life now, without them, with different challenges, joys, and sorrows. I accept that my life is on a strange and unfamiliar course, but this is where I am. My son and daughter-in-law may have taken my grandchildren from me, but I will not allow them to take away my happiness.

My life has undergone a rewrite, one that has no chapters that include my adult child and grandchildren, at this time. But despite the monumental, heartbreaking changes that have occurred, I am committed to trusting myself, letting go of fear-based beliefs, and creating harmony and equilibrium in my life. Above all, I continue to love my family and remain hopeful that one day, we will reconcile and heal all wounds and misunderstandings.

Who are you now? You are a miracle of unconditional love, because through it all, in spite of it all, incredibly and blessedly, you love them still.

> I have found the paradox, that if you love until it hurts, there can be no more hurt, only more love.
> —Mother Teresa

10. In-Laws

> I can always tell when the mother-in-law's coming
> to stay; the mice throw themselves on the traps.
> —Les Dawson

Many parents and grandparents have been alienated because of a daughter- or son-in-law.

Children grow up and go through rites of passage, and one day, they break the news that they are getting married. You're excited for them, looking forward to having a new member of the family and maybe grandchildren someday.

But unfortunately, you soon realize that you don't quite connect with your new daughter- or son-in-law. You work hard at it, but your intentions, words, and actions are often misinterpreted and criticized. You keep trying to find common ground where you can communicate effectively, but you just wind up feeling confused and uncomfortable.

That's when you start walking on eggshells.

When you look back, you recognize that there were early signs that you were on shaky ground. Maybe your daughter-in-law disapproved of a comment you made or your family wasn't invited to the pre-wedding activities. At the time, you did your best to cooperate and go with the flow. But as it turned out, these small problems were a foreshadowing of the biggest heartbreak of your life.

There are many jokes about in-laws, especially mothers-in-law.

They can be funny; for example: "I never forget a face, but in my mother-in-law's case, I'm willing to make an exception," or "Last night the local peeping Tom knocked on my mother-in-law's door and asked her to shut her blinds." But though we may chuckle, there is blatant disrespect inherent in these jokes.

It's true that it can be challenging to blend families, and it takes effort on all sides to find ways to be considerate, accepting, and gracious. But what is extremely difficult to understand is why so many of our adult children's spouses don't seem interested in communicating and just want to get rid of us altogether.

The problems with my daughter-in-law began soon after she married my son, and they became insurmountable after several years. I was expected to comply with a long list of unreasonable demands, which, after much bobbing and weaving, I could not perform to her satisfaction. The bottom line, I believe, was that she wanted me gone.

My grandchildren lost me and I them, suddenly and without any explanation. In addition, I lost the relationship I once had with my son. As the saying goes, "A son is a son until he marries," but I doubt that sentiment includes excommunicating a loving mother and grandmother for no good reason.

Being maligned by an in-law is a heartbreaking problem, with no easy solution. After doing our best to make whatever concessions and reparations necessary, but ultimately failing to come to any agreement, we parents and grandparents must then choose to start taking care of ourselves. We must practice self-respect and self-love, starting now. Otherwise, we will sink under the weight of being treated as if we are worthless and irrelevant.

> Be who you are and say what you feel because those who mind don't matter, and those who matter don't mind.
>
> —Dr. Seuss

11. Don't Take It Personally

Your son or daughter doesn't return your calls. Your future daughter-in-law doesn't seem to like you. Your son-in-law is disrespectful. Your daughter-in-law tells lies about you, and on and on it goes.

As alienated parents and grandparents, you have been mistreated, even bullied, often for unknown reasons. However, if you can possibly view your adult children's behaviors dispassionately, you will understand that they have their own perceptions, contexts, and wounds. Though you have done your best to comprehend their behavior and conveyed your willingness to work on healing the gap between you, it didn't work.

Don't take it personally.

Their behavior may come from a place inside them they may not understand, themselves. They may be unaware of the impact their actions have had on you. Maybe your adult child is being pressured by a spouse, or they may have unresolved issues they have no idea how to navigate.

Yes, you made mistakes as a parent; what parent hasn't? The healthiest approach, of course, is to listen to your adult child, accept that there is a problem, and talk it out, taking responsibility where appropriate. Unfortunately, if your child or their partner or spouse remain unwilling to forgive, communicate effectively, or let go of their grievances, you've got a no-win problem. The only way a loving, open, and mutually respectful relationship is possible is if all concerned are dedicated to its very existence and continuity.

Unless you have harmed your grandchildren in some way, the act of distancing you from them is irrational. Know that their decision to expel you from your family and deprive you and your grandchildren of the special love that exists between you is, by every measure, unconscionable. And beyond your control.

> Whatever happens around you, don't take it personally.... Nothing other people do is because of you. It is because of themselves.
> —Don Miguel Ruiz

12. Powerlessness

> Ultimately, the only power to which man should aspire is that which he exercises over himself.
> —Elie Weisel

We are powerless over others. I repeat: We are powerless over others. This includes our grown child.

At one time, we were responsible for the well-being of our child, but this is no longer the case. Our grown children are responsible for their own behaviors, attitudes, and choices. We are only responsible for ourselves: our behaviors, our attitudes, our choices. That's it.

It's paradoxical that when we seek to control other people or events, we ultimately lose our own power. But when we find the strength to let go and turn within, we find real power. The Tao Te Ching says, "Mastering others is strength. Mastering yourself is true power." This power is not ego-based but a result of experience, acquired wisdom, and humility. It's a huge relief when we recognize how powerless we really are over anyone but ourselves, because it's exhausting trying to keep track of everyone else.

It takes courage to let go and love ourselves enough to release others. The gift is that when we stand in our own inner power and release attachments to how it should be or stop saying, "I'll be happy when …," we relax and let everything be just as it is.

As misguided as our adult child's behaviors may be, we can't control them, and we only hurt ourselves when we try. We must take the separation from them on their terms. We can beat ourselves up and rail against their actions, or we can relax, surrender, and accept the reality that's right in front of us. Let's take our hands off the wheel; we're going in circles anyway, and we'll just end up tired, lost, and confused.

We can't change people. We can't control them or cure them.

The only power we have is over ourselves.

13. Stranger in a Strange Land

> Alienation: This is the feeling that you're a stranger in your own life, a stranger in the world.
>
> —Unknown

You're a grandparent who cannot see or know your grandchildren. When people ask you about your grandkids, instead of running screaming from the room, it's usually best to answer the question with something like, "My grandkids are doing great," and then change the subject.

It's difficult to be with friends who have normal relationships with their grandchildren. It can feel like you've suddenly arrived on a planet where everyone but you is part of a healthy, intact family. It doesn't seem right or fair that you have been deprived of something as natural as being an involved and loving grandparent. And as glad as you are for those who have active, happy relationships with their grandkids, you can't help but feel bereft and sad because you've been cheated out of a normal relationship with yours.

Perhaps you did everything in your power to mend the rift, like making amends, doing your best to appease and reason with your adult child, but nothing worked. Your only choice, then, is to disengage, reevaluate your life, adapt to the many changes, and forgive yourself for whatever mistakes you made as a parent.

Psychologist Jeanne Achterberg observed, "Healing is embracing what is most feared; healing is opening what has been closed, softening what has hardened into obstruction; healing is learning to trust life." It is achingly sad to be a grandparent without access to your grandchildren: a no-man's land of lost hugs and broken dreams. But time passes, and your heart heals (at least a bit). A day finally dawns when your grandchildren are not foremost in your mind. You have lunch with a friend, you laugh, you read a good book, you see a movie. Maybe later, you wake up in the night and suddenly mourn their absence, but you call to mind this recent reprieve from your grief. You realize that even though you are still suffering, you're beginning to get stronger.

You continue to feel like a stranger in your own life, but you are getting used to it. There are growing gaps in your grief. Even though you live your days in a strange and terrible land that has no grandchildren, you are beginning to experience unexpected moments of joy.

14. Missing Your Adult Child

Missing your grandchildren is an ongoing torture, but added to that is the agony of missing your own adult child, with whom you may have shared a close relationship prior to the estrangement. How does a parent cope with such a loss?

There is no way to prepare for this kind of heartbreak. Many parents and grandparents who have been kicked to the curb are forced into a position of appealing to their adult children for clarity. They implore their child to reconsider their decision to alienate them. When adult children refuse, parents experience a devastation like no other.

The big obstacle to complete healing and recovery from the anguish of abandonment by your adult children is the fact that you never stop loving them. You cradled them, held their hands when walking across a street, tickled them, felt their foreheads when they were sick, kissed their sweet faces, and watched them sleep. There is no stronger love than that of parents for their child.

Missing your grown child is a strange and terrible phenomenon. It feels like an unnatural act that they have walked away from you, often without an explanation or remorse.

C. S. Lewis wrote, "Spiteful words can hurt your feelings but silence breaks your heart." It's true. I miss the sound of my son's voice. I miss hearing him call me "Mom." From time to time, I wake up in the morning and hear the echo of his voice on the soft edge of a dream. Yet he and I walk on this earth, separately, with a thundering silence between us.

What can be done when your heart has broken and you miss your child so much, you fear you'll never be happy again, never feel whole again, and never stop grieving? Start by eliminating your use of any social media, like Facebook and Instagram, that have posts and pictures of your adult child and grandchildren. Put them out of your mind as often as you can. You simply don't need to know what they're doing in their lives, because it will only hurt you.

Find the strength to change your thoughts; tell yourself not to go there when tempted to indulge in shame or guilt. Create a mantra or affirmation that you plant in your mind and repeat over and over again (for example, "I am a loving, kind, and vibrant person, and I deserve to be treated with respect and love"). Breathe deeply, with a full inhale, followed by an even deeper exhale; get more oxygen in your system. Drink a glass of water, move your body, pray for help. Say, "Stop," when thoughts of your adult child's renunciation of you creep back into your mind, and refuse to have that conversation with yourself yet again.

You had many years of living before you became a parent. In fact, active parenting is, on average, about eighteen years per child; beyond that, you are no longer as involved with their everyday care and maintenance. There's still a lot of life left, and it can be exciting and rich. Yes, there is the dark reality of estrangement skulking in the corners of your consciousness, but using the techniques above, you can scare it off and refuse to let it overcome you. Acknowledge its existence and then turn away from it and get back to what you were doing.

Our adult children are from us and of us, flesh of our flesh. Our heartbreak is real; we will never stop missing them. We have no choice but to go on without them.

The wind is crowded with
hungry ghosts tonight.

Sitting at my kitchen table,
I warm my hands
on a mug of hot coffee.

My eyes cut to the mantle,
to the photo, where
your laughter was once caught
like a passing train.

Tears splash into the coffee,
steaming, teeming
with memories.

Where you once were,
there's barely a trace.

Oh, my son,
how I miss you.

15. Letting Go

> To let go is to release the images and emotions, the grudges and fears, the clingings and disappointments of the past that bind our spirit.
> —Jack Kornfield

If you wish to achieve a state of freedom and happiness, you must let go of any need you have to control your adult child, including the desire to be heard, loved, and respected by them.

When the estrangement I am experiencing began, I was upset by accusations that were unfounded. At first, I protested, because I couldn't admit to what was untrue, but being defensive only generated more accusations. Eventually, I found myself in a free-fall, and even then, I held on to the hope that we could all find a middle ground and go forward from there. In other words, I couldn't let go.

The Tao Te Ching says, "When I let go of what I have, I receive what I need." It became clear to me that I was creating more pain by holding on to an untenable situation. I desperately wanted to belong, to be an integral part of my family, but I now understand that I experienced a false sense of belonging. By that, I mean that I behaved in a way that I hoped would appease my daughter-in-law and thereby assure my place in the family system. But in the process, I became more and more inauthentic and troubled. By keeping a tight grip on what, in reality, made me *unhappy*, I made it impossible to be happy. When I realized the futility of this, I recognized that the only possibility for happiness would be through letting go of everything that was making me sad.

I began training my mind to focus on thoughts that were not about being estranged and missing the kids. I began to embrace change and stopped resisting the inevitable impermanence of all things. In his book *Letting Go*, David R. Hawkins writes, "Every life crisis carries within it the kernels of a reversal, a renewal, an expansion, a leap in consciousness, and a letting go of the old and a birth of the new." I wanted a new context and perspective about the events in my life, so I stopped wishing things were different and renewed my commitment to the practice of acceptance and gratitude. I worked on letting go of unhealthy attachments to people, places, and things. I removed the drama from my circumstances, which made them less overwhelming and traumatic. I learned (and am still learning) how to say, "Is that so?" or "I understand," and when I have no other choice, I let it all go.

If your adult children are unkind or unreasonable, the healthy thing to do is to separate yourself from them. Holding on to harmful emotions such as guilt and resentment only hurts and punishes *you*. Absolve yourself from guilt, and know that you did the best you could with what you knew at the time.

Refuse to let ill-treatment, disrespect, or insults colonize your mind and heart. This doesn't mean you don't love your children or have compassion for them. They may be experiencing unresolved pain and, because of this, may feel justified in disconnecting from you and alienating you from your grandchildren. You have no control over this decision. The best thing you can do is to let go, with love, and take care of yourself.

There is a saying: "Let go or be dragged." Release them. Let your child go. Rest your overworked mind, and ease your aching heart. Let all the stress melt away, and enjoy the freedom that comes from practicing and integrating the art of letting go.

Parents rarely let go of their children, so children let go of them. They move on. They move away. The moments that used to define them—a mother's approval, a father's nod—are covered by moments of their own accomplishments. It is not until much later, as the skin sags and the heart weakens, that children understand; their stories, and all their accomplishments, sit atop the stories of their mothers and fathers, stones upon stones, beneath the waters of their lives.

—Mitch Albom

16. Depression

> Mysteriously and in ways that are totally remote from natural experience, the gray drizzle of horror induced by depression takes on the quality of physical pain.
> —William Styron

Depression is a serious by-product of alienation and estrangement. It's common to feel lost and to want to stay in bed, hidden under a comforter.

I know. I've been there.

It's natural to experience this. It's part of the grieving process. You've been dealt a blow, and it takes time to find your equilibrium. Go ahead and sigh, cry, and hide. For now.

Albert Ellis, the psychologist who developed rational emotive behavior therapy, said, "You largely constructed your depression. It wasn't given to you. Therefore, you can deconstruct it."

One of the problems with depression is the tendency to ruminate, repeating the same negative thoughts, over and over, which makes everything worse. Learning to stop these damaging thoughts by getting busy with an activity or socializing with others works wonders to distract yourself, reset your mind, and lift your mood.

It is strongly suggested that you process your loss and manage your grief, ideally with the help of a therapist. In addition, there is research supporting the notion that various lifestyle changes can also help with depression. For example, daily exercise, exposure to sunlight, focusing attention on engrossing activities, choosing TV and movies carefully, generating a strong social network, getting adequate sleep, and eating a healthy diet have been proven to be effective for treating depression. In other words, do more and think less.

When you wake up in the morning, ask yourself these questions: How am I going to get above this? What can I do for myself today that is loving and kind? How many ways can I let go and accept what is? For example, making an appointment with a therapist, getting a massage, attending a class, going for a bike ride with a friend, or just invoking joy and gratitude for all the good in your life can be very helpful in moving you out of sadness.

Underlying most depression is unexpressed, internalized anger. In the words of philosopher George Santayana, "Depression is rage spread thin." But even if you are in the throes of the guilt, shame, hurt, anger, hopelessness, and grief that are by-products of depression, know that you will get through this.

The good news is that if you do the work necessary to heal, depression eventually runs its course. One day, you will get tired of your zombie hair, heavy bones, and red-rimmed eyes. You will, perhaps tentatively at first, open the window shades and let some sunshine in. You'll splash water on your face, brush your hair, and say hello to that person in the mirror because you've missed that person, you love that person, and that person deserves to get on with life.

When you're ready, you will tap into your courage, resilience, and vibrant spirit. Little by little, you'll begin to feel lighter, and you will laugh and enjoy life again.

> Negative thinking patterns can be immensely deceptive and persuasive, and change is rarely easy. But with patience and persistence, I believe that

nearly all individuals suffering from depression can improve and experience a sense of joy and self-esteem once again.

—David D. Burns

17. Shame

For so long, estrangement wasn't discussed, mostly because people were mortified about their situations. But, thankfully, we now are bringing this problem out into the open, sharing our pain and shining a light on the malignancy that alienation and estrangement is.

Many estranged parents and grandparents feel shame. We may be judged harshly by people who have normal relationships with their family members. We're confused, embarrassed, and heartbroken. We fear that we failed as parents.

Most of us know what shame feels like. We feel shame when we make mistakes, like stuttering while giving a speech or singing out of tune. Shame is behind bullying, angry outbursts, and the need to be right. Shame makes us want to hide, run away, or numb our feelings with food, alcohol, or drugs. Our hearts beat too fast; we blush and perspire when we feel shame.

Anaïs Nin wrote, "Shame is the lie someone told you about yourself." Shame often begins in childhood, when emotional wounds take root in our subconscious. When we received disapproval or reprimands from authority figures, we internalized the belief that we were inadequate. We learned to stuff our hurt, anger, and embarrassment. We traded our authenticity for approval and acceptance. We learned early on that we had to follow the rules of engagement, which meant that we must behave the way our parents, guardians, and teachers dictated. We learned that love was conditional, and when we failed to please, we experienced shame.

Personally, it has taken me a long time to identify all the shame prowling around in my subconscious. I grew up feeling inferior and self-conscious, which was profoundly damaging to my psychological health, development, and well-being. I began having panic attacks in my teens, but no one identified them as such. After much time and work, I know, now, that these problems were precipitated by a shame that had its genesis in childhood experiences.

I got married at the age of twenty, which ended in divorce seven years later, when my son was four years old. Soon after the divorce, my mother died suddenly of a brain tumor. I lost my home and job, and suffered from chronic respiratory infections. It was at this point that my ex-husband sued me for custody of our son (this predated the practice of joint custody). With the condition that I would remain as active as possible in my son's life, I agreed to allow my ex-husband temporary custody because he was in a position to offer security and stability. Even though I felt I made the best decision for the care of my child, for many years following this period in my life, I was lost and in deep grief.

I am haunted by the long-term effects all that turmoil may have had on my young child. I did everything I could to make it up to him, but, of course, it's impossible to change what happened or alter decisions I made. However, it *is* possible to change the way I think about them. As a result, I am unraveling a complex maze of false beliefs, emotional wounds, and shame, and processing the feelings that come up.

I choose to recreate my story. I choose to stop judging what I did or didn't do and accept who I was and am, unconditionally. I'm working on not blaming myself, hurting myself, or disapproving of myself. I've done plenty of that over the years, and it's time to stop. Little by little, I'm getting rid of the parasitical shame I've hosted in my body, heart, and mind for so long.

Every day, I get closer to making peace with my past. It's not easy, but I believe it can be done.

> Shame, depart, thou art an enemy to my salvation!
> —John Bunyan

18. What Does Your Soul Need?

> Put your ear down close to your soul and listen hard.
> —Anne Sexton

Since experiencing estrangement, I have spent too much time in mental and emotional overload. I've squandered too much energy on being miserable and feeling broken-hearted. For the longest time, I stopped noticing the richness all around me, the gifts and graces bestowed upon me, and the many wonders in my life.

It's common for parents and grandparents who endure the sorrows of estrangement to lose enthusiasm for everyday pleasures. For instance, when was the last time you walked on a velvety beach, watched the colors of dawn, or listened to the silence of stars? Do you make time to sit quietly and ask yourself what you yearn to do, to create, to experience? What do you need for further healing?

One warm summer night, I sat under a sliver of moon, missing my family and feeling quite forlorn. As I looked up at the soft sky, I relaxed my body and took several deep breaths.

Then I closed my eyes and thought, *I'm feeling so sad tonight. How do I heal, where do I go from here, and what am I to do?*

I sat quietly for a while, acknowledging my feelings and ultimately getting to a place of trusting that I would find my way.

Saint Teresa of Avila called the pain of heartbreak a "beautiful wound," which was considered a great spiritual blessing that could lead to transformation and wisdom. The pain of exile from your family can, through an active commitment to living your own truth, result in more resilience, greater authenticity, and a deeper relationship with your own soul. For me, the heartbreak of estrangement has also taught me to forgive those who have hurt me, love them, and let them go. And, above all, it has taught me to love and forgive myself.

Ask your soul, your heart, and your beautiful wound what it needs for healing and enlightenment. Then just listen. When you're ready, the answer will come.

> The soul always knows what to do to heal itself. The challenge is to silence the mind.
> —Caroline Myss

19. Older and Wiser

It is often said that getting older is not for sissies, and it's true. However, by making an effort to be flexible in body, mind, and spirit, we can discover the beauty of growing older and wiser.

In the West's youth-obsessed culture, old age is dreaded. We often put our elderly out to pasture because they are perceived as obsolete, with nothing left to contribute to society. We desperately need to change this paradigm and do what many Eastern cultures do, which is to extend respect and kindness to elders and recognize the important contributions they can make. Unfortunately, as abandoned parents and grandparents, we now have the added fear of being left alone in our old age.

Philosopher Martin Buber said that old age can be "glorious if one has not unlearned how to begin." To accomplish this, we must keep wonder and curiosity alive. We must access our inner fire, passion and spirit, which are always young and vibrant. We must recognize that everything is fleeting and consciously choose to practice being flexible, adaptable, and open to change.

Every action has consequences, and every thought shapes our experiences. As we get older, we begin to understand that we create suffering when we engage in black-and-white, all-or-nothing thinking. Many of us discover that by accepting how complex people are and realizing life is full of paradoxes, we usher in a new freedom.

Japanese poet Kenji Miyazawa wisely said, "We must embrace pain and burn it as fuel for our journey." We have lived long enough to know that wisdom is born from suffering. We've learned that there is strength in letting go and weakness in holding on too tightly. We have lost loved ones from illness, estrangement, and death. We have shed tears of sorrow and of joy.

We have been tested mightily, but we're still here: learning, creating, falling down, getting back up, laughing, and loving. And that's no small thing.

> Knowledge is learning something every day.
> Wisdom is letting go of something every day.
> —Zen proverb

20. Birthdays

> Fly free and happy beyond birthdays and across forever, and we'll meet now and then when we wish, in the midst of the one celebration that never can end.
>
> —Richard Bach

Every year now, when my birthday rolls around, I start hoping I will hear from my son and grandchildren. I start wondering if I'll get a call or a text. I feel a bit anxious, even though I do my best to put them out of my mind.

Birthdays are often made worse by the harsh reality of estrangement. We find ourselves in the grip of a terrible preoccupation: Will they or won't they call? Do they or don't they care about us? We hope they will call, but if they do, the conversation might be forced and uncomfortable. We are in a no-man's land of hope, anxiety, and fear.

This state of mind cannot sustain itself without harming us. By continuing to focus on our adult children's behaviors, we undermine ourselves and allow them to emotionally hold us hostage. We give them too much power. By always focusing our attention on their hurtful or erratic conduct, we are choosing to cheat ourselves out of happiness, and we slowly ruin the quality of our lives.

On your natal day, the anniversary of your birth, give yourself the gift of freedom from wanting and needing your child's attention, approval, and love. What you seek is not outside of yourself but within you. You need only your own love and approval of who you are, no one else's.

Why not have fun on your birthday? Eat cake, laugh, enjoy all the silly cards about getting older. Sociologist Robert Staughton Lynd wrote, "Most of us can remember a time when a birthday—especially if it was one's own—brightened the world as if a second sun has risen."

Gently sweep away the cobwebs spun by alienation and estrangement that have kept you trapped in heartache for so long. Enjoy yourself and be at peace with whatever happens. Relax, be happy and let your birthday feel like a "second sun" is brightening the world.

> You've heard of the three ages of man: youth, age, and you are looking wonderful.
> —Fancis Cardinal Spellman

21. Humor

> Insanity is hereditary; you get it from your children.
> —Sam Levenson

If you try hard enough, you can find humor even in the circumstances you now find yourself. It may be a bit twisted at times, but who cares, as long as it makes you laugh?

Laughter releases endorphins, the "feel good" hormones, and is an antidote to depression, with no negative side effects. Laughter also boosts the immune system and is good for your heart.

It's good to enjoy yourself and have fun. It's good to step away from the angst and sadness you've been experiencing. British poet Lord Byron said, "Always laugh when you can. It is cheap medicine." He was right. Laughter *is* cheap medicine, so think of it as therapy: a cost-effective prescription for your health and healing.

One day, when I was missing my grandchildren, a friend dropped by. As we talked about my situation, she made a rather irreverent joke about it, and we started giggling. The jokes kept coming, and we laughed until we cried. I felt so much better afterwards, and it changed my mood.

My favorite people are those who make me laugh. Poet W. H. Auden said it well: "Among those whom I like or admire, I can find no common denominator, but among those whom I love, I can: all of them make me laugh."

So lighten up. Look for the humor in situations. Be silly. Have a belly laugh. Giggle. Let milk fly out of your nose. Enjoy your life. Healthy escapism and laughter provide balm for your soul.

Laughter has kept me vibrant and resilient. I have gone through life laughing—yes, sometimes through the tears, but laughing.

Laughter has saved my life. If you let it, it just might save yours.

> Laughter is the sun that drives winter from the human face.
> —Victor Hugo

22. Compassion

Alienation from your grandchildren has been set in motion by your adult child or their spouse. It is an unspeakable loss, one that is bewildering and devastating to both grandparents and grandchildren. But let's step back and look at it from a different perspective.

We have no idea what our adult children are dealing with in their daily lives. Marriage and relationships can be difficult. When spouses demand the expulsion of their partner's parent(s) from the family system, the stress of such a dynamic makes it extremely challenging to maintain objectivity and equilibrium. But instead of chastising them for their behaviors, it is better to view them through the lens of compassion. Abolitionist Henry Ward Beecher said, "Compassion will cure more sins than condemnation."

Each of us is at a different stage in our personal evolution. A young adult can't be expected to have the wisdom of a seventy-year-old. Everyone is living a life that is unique, and our children are no different. As much as we think we know our kids, we really don't. And they really don't know us. It's impossible to know another human being completely: their thoughts, perceptions, and secrets. We parents believe that we have dominion over our adult offspring, but we do not. We only have dominion over ourselves.

Have compassion for your grown kids and understand that they are doing the best they can. You don't know what Faustian bargains they may be making or if they are suffering from misconceptions or brain-washing. If they choose to become more conscious and learn from their experiences, they will grow in wisdom, insight, and understanding. But until then, know that they have their own struggles and heartaches.

It's important to strive to live a satisfying life, with or without your adult child and grandchildren. Give yourself the gift of freedom by releasing any need you might have for them to be different from who they are. Accept the situation, move forward in your own life, and just keep loving them.

> It is a man's sympathy with all creatures that truly makes him a man. Until he extends his circle of compassion to all living things, man himself will not find peace.
> —Albert Schweitzer

23. Acceptance

After spending most of my life trying to control people, places, and things, I woke up one day exhausted, barely able to muster enough energy to get out of bed. So for most of the day, I dragged myself around the house, too enervated to even brush my teeth.

Was I sick with the flu? No. Depressed? Yes. But I'd been depressed before, so what was different this time?

It was a hopelessness, a dark despair, a smothering exhaustion. I just wanted to curl up on the sofa and retreat from the world.

"Bring everything up to the surface," suggested Indian guru Osho. "Accept your humanity, your animality. Whatsoever is there, accept it without any condemnation. Acceptance is transformation, because through acceptance awareness becomes possible."

As scary as it was, I allowed the sadness to overtake me. At one point, I had a sudden memory of myself at four years old, alone and abandoned, crying for my mother. I let myself feel all the shame, sadness, anger, and defeat that began that day and has haunted me for too long. As I wept, however, I felt a place in my heart begin to gently open.

I have feared abandonment most of my life and have unconsciously begged people to love me. When I finally understood that so much of my energy and life force had gone into looking for love, acceptance, and intimacy, my heart broke all over again. But out of the exhaustion and deep sadness I felt that day, a wonderful awakening began within me.

We know, intellectually at least, that wanting to be loved when we don't love ourselves only results in more wanting. If we look outside ourselves for love, we won't find it or even be able to fully receive it until we love ourselves. Without an inner core of self-acceptance, we will never feel whole. But when we summon and connect with our own spirit, we construct an inner stability that sustains us.

To spend a lifetime trying to control people and events causes only suffering. Things are what they are, and people are who they are. Good things happen; bad things happen. We experience joy and sorrow, ease and dis-ease, success and failure. When we learn to accept what is, we stop evaluating, comparing, and judging. We find peace.

Virginia Satir, known for her therapeutic work with families, said, "Life is not the way it's supposed to be. It's the way it is. The way you cope with it is what makes the difference." This pertains to your grown child's decision to estrange you; you are powerless to change it, and you can change only your beliefs about the situation.

Keep your heart and mind open, and make friends with the truth. Life will unfold as it will, and by accepting what *is,* you can finally find peace.

> Life is a series of natural and spontaneous changes. Don't resist them—that only creates sorrow. Let reality be reality. Let things flow naturally forward in whatever way they like.
>
> —Lao Tzu

24. Appreciation

Acknowledge and express appreciation for the people in your life who love and care about you. Take a moment to appreciate everyday blessings like shelter, clean water, and a warm comforter to snuggle under on a cold winter's night. Appreciation changes your perspective. By stepping out of judgement and criticism, you discover qualities to enjoy and honor, not just in others, but in yourself as well.

Alienation from your grandchildren, or any part of your family, is very painful, but if you consciously shift your focus and search for things to appreciate, you will feel better. For example, appreciate your health, your home, and the everyday kindnesses of friends. Appreciate the fact that your grandchildren are alive and well; as long as this is the case, there is a real possibility you may reunite with them one day.

Voltaire said, "Appreciation is a wonderful thing. It makes what is excellent in others belong to us as well." Being appreciative does not mean that we deny the pain and suffering we've endured. It doesn't mean we condone the actions of those who are responsible for the estrangement we are experiencing. It does, however, mean that we deactivate resentment, blame, and anger, and we begin to view those who have hurt us through loving eyes and with a compassionate heart. By changing our perspective from what we lack to appreciation for all that life puts before us, good and bad, we transcend our circumstances.

Nancy Lee Klune

> Even after all this time,
> the sun never says to the earth,
> "You owe me."
> Look what happens with
> a love like that.
> It lights the whole sky.
>
> —Hafiz

25. Self-Talk

> The world we have created is a product of our thinking; it cannot be changed without changing our thinking.
>
> —Albert Einstein

On average, according to the experts, we have about fifty thousand thoughts a day. Approximately 70 to 80 percent of these are negative, such as imagining worse-case scenarios, expecting failure and defeat, or fearing loss, loneliness, or rejection.

What have you been thinking about lately?

Your thoughts create your reality. If you change your thoughts, you can actually change your reality. It takes practice, but by disciplining your thoughts to be more positive and life-affirming, you can turn your life around.

Painful memories of hurtful behaviors by your adult child, anxiety about the present, or fears about the future are unwelcome gifts that just keep on giving. By revisiting the sad events of alienation, you damage yourself over and over again, until you can't find your way out of the grief. If you teach yourself to derail negative thoughts and switch to a track of supportive and constructive thoughts, you will eventually create new neural pathways in your brain and, as a result, better habits of thinking.

Looking in the mirror and saying kind, positive things to yourself is an effective tool. I have found that it's powerful to make eye contact with myself in the mirror (which was difficult at first) while saying the affirmation. Here are some examples of beneficial affirmations:

- ☐ I am at peace with all that is happening in my life because it is for my highest good.
- ☐ I am safe, healthy, and at ease. All is well.
- ☐ I am vibrantly healthy, happy, and at peace. I radiate love.
- ☐ I am protected and loved.

You can choose your own affirmations that fit your particular circumstances. Always begin with the first person in the present tense, followed by a positive statement (e.g., "I am happy."). Believe it and feel it. It's a simple practice and easily done once or twice a day for several minutes.

Become the guardian of your mind. Instead of lamenting the unfortunate reality of estrangement, you might tell yourself something like this: "I have a wonderful life. Although I miss my adult child and grandchildren very much, I can't change the way it is right now. It doesn't mean that this is forever, so in the meantime, I will do everything I can to enjoy my life. Today is a beautiful day, and I have many blessings for which I am deeply grateful."

When we tell ourselves good things, good things seem to happen. What do you have to lose except a load of negativity and grief? In the words of Tinkerbell, "Think happy thoughts."

Simple.

26. HALT

HALT is an acronym for "Hungry, Angry, Lonely, and Tired." While I was the activities director at an addiction facility, I often called upon this concept as an effective recovery tool for the clients. HALT is a method of checking in with one's levels of hunger, anger, and mood. It is a beneficial practice, helpful in preventing relapse and in dealing with alienation and estrangement.

Skipping meals and becoming too hungry affects blood sugar, which impacts mood, but is easily remedied by carrying healthy snacks and eating regularly. There is also a hunger that is emotional in nature, such as hunger for love, companionship, and support. This need is common among estranged parents and grandparents, and it deserves attention because it can be debilitating and problematic for recovery. The best solution is to find community, such as visiting a friend, attending a personal growth meeting, or getting involved in activities like tennis lessons, volunteering at a local animal shelter, or joining a book club.

Anger is a predictable, logical response to being marginalized, denigrated, and abused by our alienators. When our bodies get run down, hungry, or tired, our defenses weaken, and we may get angry and lose control more easily. If you find yourself feeling resentful or angry, take some deep breaths, excuse yourself from the stressful situation, get some rest, eat something healthy, drink a cup of tea, call a friend or therapist, or take a brisk walk.

Loneliness is also a common condition that comes out of

estrangement. We often isolate ourselves because we feel too depressed to socialize. We're just not ready to talk about the problem with others, or we can't handle seeing other grandparents enjoying a normal relationship with their grandchildren. That may be a good time to find a therapist or a support group. And connecting with loving family and friends who understand the situation is always a good idea.

"Fatigue makes cowards of us all," observed legendary coach Vince Lombardi. If we don't get enough quality sleep, we are compromised on all levels: physically, mentally, and emotionally. When we're tired, we don't think clearly, and we become emotionally vulnerable.

Personally, I have always needed at least eight hours of sleep a night. I am a light sleeper, and I need a quiet room, a just-right pillow, and a firm mattress. As I became increasingly stressed from being cut out of my grandchildren's lives, I had problems sleeping, which exacerbated my anxiety and depression. Because sleep is so vital for a healthy state of mind, I have made my bedroom a virtual sleep chamber. I relax at least an hour before going to bed, and I use my bedroom almost exclusively for sleep. I sleep like a baby now (albeit a baby with stiff joints and senior moments), and I wake up refreshed, with the energy I need to deal with the day ahead.

If you feel yourself starting to run on empty, remind yourself to stop what you're doing and remedy the situation by addressing your level of hunger, anger, loneliness, and tiredness. If all four of these conditions coincide, you have a perfect storm for a potential meltdown. The above tools will help you avoid this and reset your course in the right direction.

> To keep the body in good health is a duty ... otherwise we shall not be able to keep our mind strong and clear.
>
> —Buddha

27. Dark Night of the Soul

> Facing the darkness, admitting the pain, allowing the pain to be pain, is never easy. This is why courage—big-heartedness—is the most essential virtue on the spiritual journey.
> —Matthew Fox

When you experience estrangement, your heart feels splintered, and you lose your bearings. You walk in daylight, but you can't see the colors. You hear the music of children laughing and playing, but it only hurts your ears. You eat without tasting your food. You continue to breathe, but your breath is shallow and sighing. You dream of your loved ones and wake up, your pillow wet with tears. You feel empty, depressed, and abandoned, not only by your child but by all you hold sacred.

Maybe you've lost your spirit, your faith in life. Things look dark, occluded, foreign. The despair you feel is beyond words. People do their best to understand and support you, but it's not enough; no one can bring your family back. You read every book and article on the subject of alienation and estrangement. You try mood stabilizers, cognitive therapy, mindfulness, compartmentalization, a change of scenery, more sleep, less sleep, a walk every morning, more sunshine, vitamins, volunteer work. These are all good tactics and they may help, but if you're seeking an explanation for your adult child's behaviors do so, but don't stop there. Go deeper. Seek help, perhaps from a therapist or spiritual counselor. Pray to the God of your understanding. In the words of writer Dan Millman:

> Every positive change—every jump to a higher level of energy and awareness—involves a rite of passage. Each time to ascend to a higher rung on the ladder of personal evolution, we must go through a period of discomfort, of initiation. I have never found an exception.

I have studied the phenomena of estrangement, alienation, and abandonment for years, but the search for knowledge and a rationale for this problem left me even more confused. When I finally realized that there were no concrete answers for understanding the people involved, or their perceptions and behaviors, I chose to seek a spiritual solution. I desperately needed peace and wanted to find a light to lead me out of the darkness.

You are undergoing a transformation, a baptism by fire, an awakening. You are growing in wisdom and acceptance. In the words of Steven Covey, "Be patient with yourself. Self-growth is tender; it's holy ground. There is no greater investment."

> The dark night of the soul comes just before revelation. When everything is lost, and all seems darkness, then comes the new life and all that is needed.
>
> —Joseph Campbell

28. Getting Help

There may come a time during your recovery from estrangement when you find yourself at a dead end. You've cried a thousand tears, beseeched the heavens, and howled at the moon. You've talked and talked about your sorrows to friends and family, and you've agonized about your past, present, and future. In spite of all this, you still ache every minute of every day and can find no solace or relief.

Estrangement is extremely difficult to heal because, by its very nature, it lacks resolution or closure. You mourn the relationships you once had and are unable to have again. And even if the estrangement were to heal, the relationship will be forever changed.

Ultimately, you are left with an ongoing bereavement, with no funeral or eulogy. You are forced to grieve the death of relationships with loved ones who are alive and well.

This can be too much to process on your own. Estrangement is enormous in its ramifications, and the pain is debilitating. In addition, there is a good chance that you may be suffering from post-traumatic stress disorder due to the shock related to the estrangement. Under these circumstances, it would be wise to find a compassionate professional to help you.

There are signs along the way that indicate when seeking help from a therapist is advisable:

- ☐ You feel anxious, depressed, and hopeless most of the time.
- ☐ You cry on and off for days, weeks, or months.

- ☐ You can't sleep, or you sleep too much.
- ☐ You stay home in your pajamas for weeks at a time.
- ☐ You lose interest in hygiene, exercise, and other healthy activities.
- ☐ You can't concentrate on normal tasks and often find yourself staring into space.
- ☐ Takeout pizza has become your main food group.
- ☐ You have thought about suicide.

If you relate to any of the above list, find help and support immediately. Even though no one can fix the problem of alienation, a good therapist can listen, provide ideas for healing the trauma, and incorporate techniques for handling stress and negative thinking.

> Just as the body goes into shock after a physical trauma, so does the human psyche go into shock after the impact of a major loss.
> —Anne Grant

29. Managing Anger

There are times when we need to feel our anger. Alienated parents and grandparents have a lot to be angry about, and the healthy course is to acknowledge it, let it out, and let it go.

Anger must be released when bottled up inside. As Buddha famously said, "Holding on to anger is like grasping a hot coal with the intent of throwing it at someone else; you are the one who gets burned." Anger very often camouflages a profound sadness, grief, or powerlessness that we're terrified of feeling. And though we may be working on forgiveness and letting go of the pain of betrayal, we sometimes just want to shake our fists at the heavens above us and yell, "To hell with them!"

That's not necessarily a bad thing. Anger can be a way of honoring our dignity, keeping our self-respect, and acknowledging to ourselves that we do not, on any level, deserve the treatment we received from our adult child. Righteous anger is a healthy response to morally objectionable behavior and can be used to create healthier boundaries. Gloria Steinem said it well: "The truth will set you free, but first it will piss you off."

One day, after a very upsetting communication with my son and daughter-in-law, I was so frustrated and angry that I thought I'd go crazy if I didn't figure out a way to release it. I cried and screamed into a pillow, and then I rolled up a towel and hit it against a concrete wall until I was worn out. It helped quite a bit, and as I calmed down, I took deep breaths and told myself that I would be okay.

Chronic, unexpressed anger can affect your health, increase anxiety, cause sleep difficulties, and lead to compulsive behaviors. If you decide to release your anger, find a safe environment where you can yell into a pillow or punch a cushion; you don't want to get in touch with your rage while driving a car or putting away the dishes. Be careful not to hurt yourself or anyone else. And don't scare your pet, if you have one. Safely discharge your anger as explained above, or find a way that works for you, like running or just jumping up and down.

As you wind down from venting your anger, take a few deep breaths to calm yourself. You may feel the need to cry, so allow your tears to flow freely; there is healing in the releasing of tears. Soothe yourself, and know that it is a courageous act to feel your anger and do the work to set it—and yourself—free.

It is important to learn how to not only discharge anger but also manage it. For example, if you feel yourself getting angry, take several slow, deep breaths. Stop for a moment and compose yourself before saying anything. If that's not possible, take a time-out, take a walk, or go to the gym and do a strenuous workout. If appropriate, use humor to deflect the stress and tension. And have a forgiving heart, because if you hold a grudge, you will just get angrier. Finally, if you feel you have a problem with rage and anger, you might consider an anger management support group.

You may not be able to control the situation you're in, but you *can* control what you do with your feelings. By managing instead of suppressing anger, it will no longer control you.

> Anger ventilated often hurries toward forgiveness; and concealed often hardens into revenge.
> —Edward G. Bulwer-Lytton

30. Ups and Downs

One morning, you wake up, and your heart is racing; your thoughts are going around in circles. You're thinking about your adult child, your grandchildren, and all that has happened. You're sad about the past, anxious about the present, and fearful about the future. You can't believe you've fallen back down into that emotional abyss, especially since you've been doing so much better lately.

Experience will teach you to expect these sudden onsets of anxiety and flashbacks of painful events, which are common symptoms of post-traumatic stress disorder. You've learned coping strategies, such as how to switch gears and change your thoughts. So you take some deep breaths, do a couple of stretches, maybe say a prayer or an affirmation, and then get out of bed and make some strong coffee to help lift your mood.

Healing from the pain of estrangement is fraught with ups and downs. It's unpredictable and exhausting. It's important to remember that just around the corner could be another emotional boulder. There are countless dangers, such as a sudden painful memory or the occasion of a grandchild's birthday party, graduation, or wedding to which you haven't been invited. Just when you think it's safe to relax your vigilance, you get hit with a sudden setback. Even though you've experienced this before, you're stunned, nevertheless. You're surprised you're still vulnerable, still hurting, still angry, still deeply sad after all this time.

American Buddhist Pema Chödrön wrote, "Nothing ever goes

away until it has taught us what we need to know." So what do we need to know? We need to know how to compartmentalize by putting aside images we may have inside our head of the heartaches we've endured and replace them with happier images. We need to guard against negativity and self-sabotage. We need to pay attention to our environment, know our limits, and entertain only thoughts that give us relief. We need to practice acceptance and make peace with the reality that there will always be ups and downs, gains and losses, pleasure and pain, sadness and joy.

And we need to do everything we can to avoid a tumble down into the pit of despair. We've already fallen in enough times to know that it only prolongs the pain.

> When you get into a tight place and everything goes against you, till it seems as though you could not hold on a minute longer, never give up then, for that is just the place and time that the tide will turn.
> —Harriet Beecher Stowe

31. Self-Soothing

A natural response to the extreme anxiety brought on by estrangement is overstimulation of the amygdala, which is the part of the brain that processes emotions. Due to constant stress, loss, and trauma, the brain becomes habituated to a state of high alert. It's important to defuse this response and calm down. Since we can't always get in touch with a therapist, health practitioner, friends, or family, we can learn to help ourselves when we are in need of comfort. We can self-soothe. It can be as simple as taking a moment to walk outside and look up at the sky, or taking a slow, deep breath and saying, "Peace before me, peace behind me, peace above me, peace below me, peace within me, peace all around me."

I have made a list of some practices that I have found helpful:

Therapeutic Activities

- ☐ Light a candle, put on soft, comfortable clothing, and sip something warm.
- ☐ Listen to soothing music.
- ☐ Find something funny to read, listen to, or watch and laugh.
- ☐ Clean out a drawer or a closet (yes, I find this soothing).
- ☐ Take a hot bath.
- ☐ Use a diffuser and fill your environment with lovely, relaxing aromas from essential oils.
- ☐ Hug friends and loved ones whenever you see them.

- ☐ Walk in nature.
- ☐ Express your feelings by drawing, writing, or moving to music.

Mental/Emotional Exercises

- ☐ Believe that your life has meaning.
- ☐ Say a prayer or an affirmation, like "My life is beautiful, and I'm blessed to have so much good in my life."
- ☐ Remember that you are loved.
- ☐ Learn to revel in the contemplative quiet of aloneness.
- ☐ Know that you have worth and your life has value.
- ☐ Practice gratitude.
- ☐ Simply place your hands over your heart and breathe in love for yourself.
- ☐ Thank yourself and your courageous spirit for all you've been through.

This is by no means an exhaustive list, and what is soothing for one person may not work for another. For me, whenever it rains, I go to a room in my house where I can hear the rain on the roof, and I snuggle up with my dog and a warm blanket, close my eyes, and just listen. The rain is music to my ears, and I am able to find comfort and peace.

Soothe your nervous system on a daily basis. Discover your own ways of introducing calming distractions that are uniquely effective for *you*.

Estrangement can take a toll on every aspect of your life. Finding peace and comfort will help you become more grounded, balanced, healthier, and happier.

> There are days I drop words of comfort on myself
> like falling leaves and remember that it is enough
> to be taken care of by myself.
> —Brian Andreas

32. Mindful Moments

It's not easy to live in the present. Recently, I had a phone call from my niece, and several times while chatting with her, I found myself wondering when I would see her again. I thought about how much I miss her and wished we lived closer to each other. It wasn't until we said our goodbyes that I realized that, by thinking about what I didn't have and wishing circumstances were different, I had cheated myself out of being fully present and purely enjoying the conversation. Novelist James Baldwin wrote, "There is never time in the future in which we will work out our salvation. The challenge is in the moment; the time is always now." Since that call from my niece, I've been training myself to be more mindful of the present moment.

Are your days filled with the distractions of smartphones, texting, and social media? Do you multitask to the point of oblivion? Do you habitually poison your mind with loveless thoughts about yourself and others?

When you get caught up in day-to-day diversions, just stop. Reset your thoughts and come back to the present. For example, when you sit down to eat, savor the food and be grateful for the nourishment it gives; when you walk, feel the earth beneath your feet grounding and supporting you. Find the sacred in an ordinary day, an ordinary moment. Keep returning to your breath, as you gently remind yourself to just be here, right where you are, in all its richness and beauty.

Early in the journey you wonder how long the journey will take and whether you will make it in this lifetime. Later you will see that where you are going is HERE and you will arrive NOW ... so you stop asking.

—Ram Dass

33. Surrendering

Surrender is trust that there is a power greater than you, helping and supporting you. It is trust that all is in order, that there is a rhyme and a reason for the events in your life. It is trust that by embracing your challenges, you open the door to growth, wisdom, and a spiritual solution that exists above the level of the problem. It is making the choice to have faith and to let go of resentments and anger. In the words of Deepak Chopra, "Surrender is faith that the power of love can accomplish anything even when you cannot foresee the outcome."

Before I fully understood that surrender would be my salvation, I acted out of weakness and fear. I was desperately afraid of losing my grandchildren, afraid of being mistreated, afraid of being cast out of the family system. But as I became exhausted from all the turmoil and stress, I stopped trying to control people, places, and things and focused on my own life. I let go and surrendered to the reality of my situation.

Anne Morrow Lindberg said, "If you surrender completely to the moments as they pass, you live more richly those moments." When we release attachments to how things should be, we relax and become fully present. We experience mental, emotional, and spiritual growth. We discover a new freedom.

Trust that you are protected and guided. Trust that all is well, and let go of any need to manipulate specific outcomes. As painful as it is to be estranged from your loved ones, trust that you are right where you need to be for your own growth. Pray for the highest good of all, and surrender to what each moment brings you.

> Better still is surrender of attachment to results, because there follows immediate peace.
> —Bhagavad Gita

34. Stuck in the Victim Role

> In the long run, we shape our lives, and we shape ourselves. The process never ends until we die. And the choices we make are ultimately our own responsibility.
>
> —Eleanor Roosevelt

Most of us feel like victims of circumstances at some point in our lives. After being alienated and estranged, it's natural to feel victimized; we feel rejected, dejected, and sorry that we somehow failed our adult child. Since our previous attempts at communication yielded nothing in the way of bridging the gap between the parties involved, we feel impotent and silenced.

Whatever choices we make in life, there are payoffs. What are the payoffs for staying in the role of victim?

- ☐ We get to feel that we're right and they are wrong.
- ☐ We get to be martyrs.
- ☐ We make excuses, fail to take responsibility for our part, blame our past for the way we are, and find fault with others.
- ☐ We have an ongoing pity party, where we complain about our circumstances and whine when things don't go our way.
- ☐ We feel sorry for ourselves and vacillate between feeling put upon by others and feeling like a loser.

In the wise words of Eckhart Tolle, "To complain is always nonacceptance of what is. It invariably carries an unconscious negative charge. When you complain, you make yourself into a victim. When you speak out, you are in your power."

Being in the victim mind-set for too long becomes a bad habit. I became so tired of being helpless, hopeless, and stuck, I came up with a list of ways to help move me out of feeling victimized. If you, too, are tired of feeling like a victim of your circumstances, the following suggestions may help you make a shift:

- ☐ Decide to change your thinking. Start with small challenges, like focusing on and being grateful for the good in your life.
- ☐ Take responsibility when necessary.
- ☐ Forgive yourself and everyone else, no exceptions.
- ☐ Practice acceptance; if you can change the situation, great. If not, accept it and let it go.
- ☐ Free yourself from being affected by what others say and do. Honor your own processes, feelings, and perceptions. Empower yourself.
- ☐ Change your perspective from victim to survivor. A victim is stagnant and self-pitying, while a survivor finds the lessons inherent in the problem and keeps going with optimism and a sense of purpose.
- ☐ When you hear yourself complaining, just stop. Complaining makes everything worse and perpetuates feelings of impotence and hopelessness.
- ☐ Don't believe everything you tell yourself. Question your assertions and make corrections in your thinking. For example, if you dwell on the worst-case scenario, switch to considering what the *best*-case scenario might be like.
- ☐ Choose happiness. Make changes that are within your control, and start thinking in a positive way.

- ☐ Remind yourself, every day, that you are loved and that your life is worth living, even without your adult child and grandchildren.
- ☐ Decide that today is the day you will cancel your pity party. Get rid of shame, eliminate blame, and clean up the mess.

So no more brooding. Get in touch with and deal with your hurt, resentment, and anger. Make a choice for personal power and integrity, and step out of the victim role.

No more excuses.

> Never be bullied into silence. Never allow yourself to be made a victim. Accept no one's definition of your life; define yourself.
> —Harvey Fierstein

35. Being Happy Anyway

During the time you have been estranged, have you ever found yourself feeling better for a time, maybe even a bit lighthearted, when suddenly the dark reality of your estrangement descends into your consciousness, unbidden, blocking out any joy or happiness? You had momentarily forgotten about the alienation from your family, only to fall back into the turmoil and sadness of it all. The unfortunate reality is that this place of sadness is all too familiar now, too comfortable, too numbing.

Motivational speaker Robert Anthony said, "Most people would rather be certain they're miserable, than risk being happy." If it goes on too long, unhappiness becomes habitual. Habits, particularly bad ones, are often hard to break, but it's entirely possible to replace them with better ones.

One evening, I joined friends for dinner. We were laughing and having a wonderful time when a family came into the restaurant with four kids about the same ages as my grandchildren. It was a painful reminder of how much I missed my grandchildren, and my heart contracted. But I made a decision not to let my sadness ruin the evening. So I took a deep breath, refocused on the evening with my friends, pushed the pain aside, and let it go. I compartmentalized my problems and redirected my attention, which worked well, allowing me to come back to the present and enjoy myself.

It's up to you whether you choose to hold on to your sadness or decide to release it and enjoy your life. Being unhappy certainly won't help you, and it will only engender more unhappiness. Making a conscious effort to experience joy will strengthen your mind and mood, and, before you know it, you will have formed a new habit, one of happiness.

Even though you have experienced deep sorrow due to estrangement, you're allowed to be happy anyway. You *deserve* to be happy. Find ways to enjoy your life. It will only make things better.

> Find a place inside where there's joy, and the joy will burn out the pain.
> —Joseph Campbell

36. The Present

> This a wonderful day. I've never seen this one before.
> —Maya Angelou

Each day we live on this earth is indescribably dear. Life is a miracle, a mystery, a privilege. We too often take it for granted and forget the fact that this day will never come again.

What did you have for breakfast today? Was it healthy? How are you spending the day? Are you using your talents? Are you enriching your life and the lives of others? Are you having fun?

Decide what's important today. Do you really want to get a botox injection for that little wrinkle on your forehead? Do you really want to watch the news with so much negativity? Instead, why not look in the mirror and love your reflection, even with that tiny furrow between your brows. Call a friend who needs your support, or choose to watch a movie or read a book that makes you laugh.

Living in the present changes your perspective. You are at one with the truth that everything is temporary and ultimately disappears like a dream. In the words of Wayne Dyer, "Stop acting as if life is a rehearsal. Live this day as if it were your last. The past is over and gone. The future is not guaranteed."

Where you focus your attention will determine how you feel. Even though you might be caught up in the ordeal of alienation, you can put it aside, at least for a while, and enjoy just being alive. Life can be joyful, even in the face of tragedy.

At one point in the estrangement from my son and daughter-in-law, I realized that I was spending too much time licking my wounds. I constantly thought about the past and feared the future. I came close to letting the situation break me. One day, however, I became impatient with all the worry and sadness I'd been indulging in, and I put the brakes on harmful rumination. I came back to the here and now, and I looked around me. I noticed the fragrance of the beautiful bouquet of roses on my dining room table, the glorious music of birds singing outside my window, and the lovely sight of the morning sun creating a pattern on my kitchen ceiling. I was fully present, enjoying the moment, and it was sublime.

Feel the sun on your face, sing a song, spin around in a circle, buy an ice cream cone, ride a bicycle, climb a tree, become a falconer, learn the hula, have a wilderness adventure; why not? You only have this one life, and every moment is rich with possibilities.

> You must live in the present, launch yourself on every wave, find your eternity in each moment.
> —Henry David Thoreau

37. Turnaround Thoughts

If you are estranged from your adult child, or any part of your family, it's understandable to frame it as a disaster. By reacting reflexively, your body, mind, emotions, and nervous system are repeatedly assaulted by this negative perspective, resulting in more suffering and misery.

As difficult as it is, however, it is possible to change the nature of your thoughts about your circumstances, thereby facilitating better physical, mental, and emotional health.

Byron Katie, who teaches a process of inquiry that gets to the bottom of thought processes and how they hurt and mislead people, explains: "I discovered that when I believed my thoughts, I suffered, but that when I didn't believe them, I didn't suffer, and that this is true for every human being. Freedom is as simple as that. I found that suffering is optional. I found a joy within me that has never disappeared, not for a single moment. That joy is in everyone, always."

I have found turnaround thoughts to be quite helpful. When my thoughts start swirling with memories of past hurts, present concerns, or fears for the future, I use a turnaround thought. For example, when I recently despaired that I would never reconcile with my adult child and his wife, my turnaround thought was, *Is this really true? The future is unknown, and I choose to believe that everything is as it needs to be right now and that it will all work out for the best.*

When I find myself missing my grandchildren, I again use a turnaround thought, such as, *Of course, I miss them, but one day we may meet again. Life can change in an instant.* I have found that when I choose thoughts and beliefs that support me, I am much happier.

It does no good to dwell on the negative and be buried alive beneath the heavy weight of anger, grief, and sadness. Choose to focus only on thoughts and beliefs that nourish and support you.

> Don't waste yourself in rejection, nor bark against
> the bad, but chant the beauty of the good.
> —Ralph Waldo Emerson

38. Keeping It Simple

> What do you like doing best in the world, Pooh? [asked Christopher Robin.] "What I like best in the whole world is Me and Piglet going to see You, and You saying 'What about a little something?' and Me saying, 'Well, I shouldn't mind a little something, should you, Piglet,' and it being a hummy sort of day outside, and birds singing."
> —A. A. Milne, *The House at Pooh Corner*

One way to manage the chaos brought on by alienation and estrangement is to simplify your life by eliminating physical, mental, and emotional clutter. "Progress is discovering what you can do without," said author Marty Rubin. Too much stuff can clog your home, distract you mentally, and keep you stuck by holding on too tightly to what you no longer need.

To begin the process, start with your physical environment. Clean out closets, drawers, and cabinets. If you haven't used something in a year, get rid of it. Donate clothes you haven't worn in a long time and old pots or dishes, and toss stale spices that have been in the cabinet too long. Give away or throw away those things you think you might come in handy one day.

Sift through any pictures of your grandchildren, keepsakes, cards, or drawings from them, and as you do this, check into your feelings: If you feel sad when you look at these things, save them, but put them out of sight for now. Go through photos of your estranged child, and spend some time looking at pictures that validate you as a loving parent who did all you could with what you had to give. It might be an emotional experience, but worth the time and attention so that you can focus on memories of the good times. If there are any pictures that sadden you, put them away or throw them away. Overall, by decluttering your physical environment, you create space, increasing what the Chinese call *chi*, which means "good energy."

Next, purge your mind by getting rid of old, self-defeating thoughts. Challenge your perceptions and beliefs. Don't give credence to everything you tell yourself, and use turnaround thoughts if necessary (refer to the chapter on turnaround thoughts). Pare down expectations, especially when it comes to your adult child and grandchildren, and do what you need to do to be happy.

When I became aware of how much my brain and emotions were working overtime, I began taking several minutes every day to consciously let go of worry and anxiety. When my thoughts start spinning around, I stop what I'm doing and take several slow, deep breaths as I relax my neck and shoulders and anywhere else I'm holding tension. I come back to the moment and only think of that— not the past, not the future—and focus on it with each breath. I say thank you for this day.

Rediscover the simple joys of life. Look up at clouds, find refreshment from everyday pleasures, like sharing a meal with a good friend or feeling the warmth of the summer sun on your shoulders, and take the time to simply enjoy the "hummy sort of day outside, and birds singing."

39. Music

> Where words fail, music speaks.
> —Hans Christian Andersen

Music is basic to our experience as human beings. As children, we loved the sounds around us: rattles, clanging pots and pans, pat-a-cake, and soft lullabies. It's in our DNA to respond to melodies and rhythms.

Music can be cathartic. Studies prove that music helps people deal with the aftermath of trauma. It can help relieve anxiety and stress. It can help us relax and give us a tool for releasing emotions.

I studied music therapy and later practiced it as a therapist. I learned that when patients are sad, playing upbeat, happy music can be counterproductive, because it often results in agitating them. Instead, it's more effective, especially for therapeutic purposes, to play music that matches the mood of the patients, as it helps them process their emotions.

There have been times in my life when music saved me. I am a classical pianist, and more than once, I deliberately chose to play music that was melancholic. As I played, I went deep into my sadness and allowed myself to feel what was in my heart and soul. Maya Angelou describes it beautifully: "Music was my refuge. I could crawl into the space between the notes and curl my back to loneliness." So if you're feeling sad, you might, in a safe, supportive environment, play or listen to sad music for the purpose of catharsis.

Music is a good prescription for lowering blood pressure and slowing the heart rate and respiration. Classical music, Celtic harp music, and yoga chants are meditative and renewing. If you have trouble sleeping, playing lullabies can help improve sleep quality and duration.

Plato said, "Music gives a soul to the universe, wings to the mind, flight to the imagination and life to everything." Music can lift you up, like playing rock 'n' roll while doing housework or dancing to it just for the fun of it. You might consider singing in a chorus, joining a drum circle, or learning to play an instrument. Singing, playing an instrument, dancing, and creating music are all healing and beneficial.

Music can be a great tool for your recovery.

> Music is nourishment, a comforting elixir. Music multiplies all that is beautiful and of value in life.
> —Zoltan Kodaly

40. Healthy Self-Respect

> Parents who are afraid to put their foot down usually have children who step on their toes.
>
> —Proverb

Too often, during the distressing events that ultimately led to our estrangement, I allowed myself to become disempowered. I was repeatedly in the down position, with my alienators in the up position.

What does it mean to be in the down position? It means that you become a supplicant, petitioning for any scrap of attention, approval, or kindness that is tossed your way. In the case of a potential estrangement, you feel misunderstood, are impotent, and experience debilitating fear: fear that your world is falling apart and your can't catch all the pieces.

What would it mean if you found a way to move into an up position? Instead of invalidating yourself, you would honor yourself and protect your heart. You would come from a place of integrity, wisdom, and self-empowerment. You would not allow yourself to be abused. In the words of Helen Keller, "Never bend your head. Always hold it high. Look the world straight in the face."

When I was a child, I was often shamed, neglected, and left alone by my parents. As a result, I had very little self-esteem growing up, and I developed many insecurities and fears. I believe that if I had learned confidence and had a healthy self-respect, I would have done many things differently in my life, especially when it came to coping with the prospect and ultimate outcome of estrangement. When I was scapegoated by my son and daughter-in-law, rather than exercising healthy boundaries by agreeing to only that which was reasonable and sane, I let myself be mistreated. I had to accept the unacceptable. It saddens me that I experienced this, but I learned many priceless lessons.

Be confident and believe in yourself. Ram Dass said, "Your problem is you're too busy holding onto your unworthiness." Value yourself, your time, your experiences, your heart. You really do need to be your own best friend.

41. Mother's Day

Alienated and estranged mothers and grandmothers all agree that Mother's Day is a very painful holiday. Throughout the day, we often have a pit in the stomach and an ache in the heart. We wonder if we'll get a call, a text, a card, maybe even a miracle of flowers delivered. Or maybe radio silence.

It seems that everywhere we look, there are flower displays, Mother's Day advertisements, and restaurants swarming with families consisting of a beaming mother surrounded by her kids and grandkids. It would take a very strong estranged mother to not feel longing and sadness about her own circumstances.

Author Janet Lanese, who wrote about grandparenting, stated, "All a grandmother wants is her family's love and respect as a productive individual who has much to contribute." The privilege of being loved and honored by family has been taken from those who have been alienated and estranged, often for reasons unknown, unfair, or incomprehensible. But whether your family perceives you as someone worthy of love or not is unimportant. What is important is that *you* believe that you are lovable, productive, and valuable, with much to contribute, if not directly to your family, then to others who will benefit from your presence in their lives.

In my case, the longer the estrangement goes on, the more ambivalence I feel about Mother's Day. Each year seems a little sadder, a little more absurd. I miss my son. I am missing the childhoods of my grandchildren: the laughs, the fun, the small adventures. I've

Banished

missed hugging them and loving them from the pure, open place in my heart I hold just for them. And they have missed out, also, although they may not know it yet. But there's not a damned thing I can do about it.

Novelist Margaret Drabble has an interesting perspective: "Family life itself, that safest, most traditional, most approved of female choices, is not a sanctuary: It is, perpetually, a dangerous place." It's true that we mothers and grandmothers place enormous importance on our families and our roles as mothers (maybe too much). There have been so many Mother's Days when I wept and railed at the sky, feeling cheated and enraged. Finally, I reached a point when I refused to be defeated by circumstances and realized that the only way out of the pain was to change my attitude and perspective. I was sick to death of living with disappointment and intermittent, overwhelming grief. I made a conscious effort to let go of feelings of guilt and any negative beliefs I held about myself. I stopped letting my son, or anyone else, invalidate me. I had made amends, beaten my chest, and said mea culpa enough.

Now, on Mother's Day, I choose to celebrate that many years ago, I gave birth to a healthy baby boy I will always love and forever carry in my heart. But even more importantly, I celebrate that I am a person of worth.

> The heart of a mother is a deep abyss at the bottom of which you will always find forgiveness.
> —Honore de Balzac

42. Nourishing Your Mind

> We are shaped by our thoughts; we become what we think. When the mind is pure, joy follows like a shadow that never leaves.
>
> —Buddha

Do you ever get tired of your thought processes? Are they running rampant, keeping you hostage to anger, hurt, shame, grief, or fear?

Every thought creates a reaction. I write about this a lot because of the vital importance of learning how to change unwholesome habits of negative thinking. For example, when you have an upsetting thought, acknowledge it but refuse to indulge it. Mentally look away and choose a different thought that gives you strength and comfort. This de-energizes the unwanted thought and energizes the preferred thought. For example, when I find myself missing the relationship I once had with my son, I switch my thought to appreciating another relationship that brings me happiness, such as one I enjoy with a dear friend who always makes me laugh. I sometimes add an affirmation, such as, "I love my life. I am a loving person, and I am loved and cherished by many wonderful people."

Be vigilant in monitoring your thoughts. When you experience a negative thought, quickly say, "Cancel, delete," and replace that thought with a positive one. For example, appreciate who you are and recognize all that's good and worthy about you. Think of what you are grateful for and what puts a smile on your face. Make this a daily practice. Like nourishing your body with healthy food, nourish your mind with positive thoughts for optimum vitality and well-being.

Read. Keep your mind sharp by memorizing a poem, your shopping list, or people's names. Acquire new skills, like learning a language or a musical instrument. Be curious about the world around you. Revisit your dreams, your forgotten desires, and your passions. Create a bucket list, and fill your mind with images of intoxicating beauty, exciting adventures, and fun. Change is good for your brain and even better for your soul.

From time to time, take a break and empty your mind. Rest. Be silent and listen to your spirit. By disciplining your mind and choosing your thoughts carefully, you will begin to ease the pain in your heart. You may still be aware of your hurts, but you'll also feel a new joy stirring within you.

> The one thing that you have that nobody else has is you. Your voice, your mind, your story, your vision. So write and draw and build and play and dance and live only as you can.
> —Neil Gaiman

43. The Importance of Play

> We are never more fully alive, more completely ourselves, or more deeply engrossed in anything than when we are playing.
>
> —Charles Schaefer

When was the last time you rode a bike, drew a picture, played cards with friends, swung on a swing, giggled, juggled, spun a yo-yo, walked barefoot on the beach, roasted marshmallows, skipped down the street, or wore a silly hat to the grocery store? When was the last time you took a day off just to *play*?

My dog loves to play. He follows me around with his ball and plays keep-away or hide-and-go-seek. He's so happy when I play with him. It's same for us two-legged animals: We're happy when we play.

According to play researcher Brian Sutton-Smith, the opposite of play is not work; it's depression. What happens when we play? We're in the moment. We laugh. Our troubles recede into the background, and we feel happier and healthier overall. We are creative, unfettered. We use our energy in a different way, and, very importantly, we relax. We give our overworked brains a rest by focusing on something that gives us pleasure and release.

We may have to relearn how to play by getting in touch with the little kid who is still inside us and wants to come out and play. Many of us adults have tamped down our natural instincts for fun because of the innumerable challenges, disappointments, and heartaches we have encountered in our lives. Even so, I believe it's extremely important to engage in play as we grow older because of its profound benefits.

If you're a grandparent who is blocked from seeing or knowing your grandchildren, you undoubtedly miss playing with them. But you can find other ways to have fun, other people to play with. Pick a day and focus on having fun and sharing laughs with others. Sing along to the music in an elevator; stand on a sidewalk and look up, and see how many people also look up. Play. Be lighthearted. Goof off.

My dog loves to play, anytime, with anybody. He likes everyone and is always in the moment, happily wagging his tale, having a blast.

What a great role model.

44. Managing Moods

It is very important to stay balanced in body, mind, and spirit. As an estranged parent and grandparent, you are under tremendous stress and may be susceptible to mood swings and periods of helplessness and depression. But if you have physical, mental, and emotional compensators in place, you increase your chances of staying in a neutral zone where you can maintain your health and well-being.

On a physical level, there are many ways to keep your equilibrium, such as eating regular meals, staying hydrated, exercising, getting enough sleep, and managing any pain you might have. You can get a massage, acupuncture, or chiropractic help. You can attend a yoga class, interact with a pet, or just go outside and enjoy nature.

On a mental level, you must train your mind and discipline your thoughts on a daily basis. It is helpful to practice repeating affirmations and being in the moment. For distraction, you could read an engrossing book or watch a funny show and laugh; laughter helps everything. Talk to a friend who understands.

On an emotional and spiritual level, you might try meditation or prayer. Be silent for several minutes, close your eyes, breathe slowly and deeply, and just listen to the sounds around you. Express gratitude for all that you are and all that you have. Remember that everything—your mood, this day, this feeling—is temporary and will pass.

Many years ago, I was a professional dancer. One day, there was an audition for dancers to be cast in an NBC TV special. It was a hot, smoggy day in Burbank, California, where I lived, and my thoughts ran something like, *Why bother going? There will be hundreds of dancers competing for the job.* But then I thought, *Nothing ventured, nothing gained.* So I started singing a song from *Cabaret*, with the lyrics: "What good is sitting alone in your room? Come hear the music play!" I got up, put on my leotard and tights, and dashed out the door to the audition. I'll never forget what a huge lesson that was for me about controlling my moods and having a positive attitude, because guess what? I got the job! I danced with Lucille Ball, and it was fantastic.

So how does this apply to alienation and estrangement? It's simple: By taking risks, stretching ourselves, and having a positive, hopeful outlook, we can improve our mood, which will more readily bring about desired outcomes. We will feel lighter and have a lot more fun.

> The trick is to be grateful when your mood is high and graceful when it is low.
> —Richard Carlson

45. Thanksgiving

Over the years, estranged parents and grandparents who read my blog (www.grandparentsdeniedaccess.com) have written to me expressing sadness about missing their adult children and grandchildren at Thanksgiving. One estranged grandmother wrote that she found herself resenting all the "happy, happy people and their happy families." Her perception was that everyone was happy but her, and she was upset that she would be spending Thanksgiving alone.

As attractive as the Norman Rockwell images of the holidays may be, many of us can't relate. There is so much hype about the holidays that everywhere we look, we see idealized images of families hugging one another and laughing with good cheer. Add to that the ubiquitous movies and sentimental TV commercials, and we're tempted to run and hide under the nearest autumn-themed throw. In reality, many family gatherings are quite stressful, due to undercurrents of dysfunction, unhealed wounds, and unresolved resentments.

Many people spend Thanksgiving alone or as an add-on for dinner at a friend's house. Homeless people eat turkey dinners at soup kitchens, mentally ill people forage for food from dumpsters, and abandoned elders eat microwaved dinners in front of their TVs. As lovely as Thanksgiving is, it can be a sad and lonely day for many.

As I write this, it is Thanksgiving morning. I decided that I would say, "Thank you," for everything today. Looking out my window, I give thanks for the winter wonderland I see; I look up and am thankful for the mystical gray sky. I walk into the kitchen, make coffee, and am thankful for my effortless mobility and for the wonderful aroma. It is an excellent exercise to be thankful for everything because gratitude perpetuates itself.

I find that the holiday season is a good time to go within to that perfect place in my heart where I am whole, quiet, and accepting. It's simple: All is as it is. I remind myself that my happiness does not depend on how many people are sitting at my Thanksgiving dinner table, but rather on what I'm telling myself about my circumstances. The only way to be at peace is to be thankful for what *is* and stop comparing and let go of expectations of what I think the holidays *should* be. I know I have the power within me to enjoy this season, if I make up mind to do so.

Every Thanksgiving, as I give thanks for my many blessings, I pray for the poor, the homeless, the disabled, the lost, and the lonely. I pray for my loved ones and for all parents and grandparents whose families have been torn asunder by alienation, abandonment, and estrangement.

> What if, today, we were grateful for everything?
> —Charles Schultz, *Peanuts*

46. Morning and Evening Rituals

Mornings and evenings can be tough for estranged parents and grandparents. It's not uncommon to wake up with feelings of sadness, loneliness, or despair. Getting a good night's sleep can also be challenging due to anxiety and obsessive rumination. To help with these issues, I started practicing several simple morning and evening rituals. The morning rituals help to clear out brain fog and improve mood, while the evening rituals induce a state of deep relaxation and facilitate sleep.

Morning

- ☐ Upon awakening, feel gratitude for a new day and fresh beginnings.
- ☐ Slowly stretch and take some deep breaths. Focus on this for several minutes.
- ☐ Let go of worry and remind yourself that you can't control everything, and trying to only causes stress.
- ☐ Go over the events you've planned for the day, people you will encounter, and anticipated success and happy outcomes.
- ☐ Say the Serenity Prayer: "God, grant me the serenity to accept the things I cannot change, the courage to change the things I can, and the wisdom to know the difference."
- ☐ Rise up, smile, and look forward to your day.

Evening

- ☐ After you get in bed, lie comfortably and take several deep breaths.
- ☐ Recount the events of your day and be thankful.
- ☐ Send love to your children, grandchildren, and loved ones.
- ☐ Put your hands over your heart and give love to yourself.
- ☐ Take several more deep breaths and relax all your muscles.
- ☐ Silently say an affirmation like, *I am now safe and at peace. All is well.*

The most efficient way to live reasonably is every morning to make a plan of one's day and every night to examine the results obtained.

—Alex Carrel

47. Giving Back

> Be a lifeboat or a ladder, help someone's soul heal.
> Walk out of your home like a shepherd.
> —Rumi

If you are experiencing estrangement from a family member, you are no doubt facing hardship and pain. However, these challenges can potentially be transformative by prompting you to tap into your courage, strength, and compassion.

Finding meaning in the midst of the shock and heartbreak of alienation and estrangement is a formidable task. But it is entirely possible, and with time, as your efforts to survive and thrive yield results, you will discover peace and happiness. Your circumstances may not fit the picture of what you had once dreamed they would be, but you will achieve a new level of acceptance, vitality, and wisdom. And, surprisingly, you may have a desire to share what you've learned as a result of your experiences.

When you feel depressed, hurt, or despairing, find a way to transcend your emotions and state of mind. For example, you might join or start a support group in which you share what helped you during your healing process. You might volunteer at an animal shelter, deliver meals on wheels, help someone with their grocery shopping, hold an elevator door, start a blog, or lovingly support a friend in need.

Author Mary S. Edgar expressed it well: "I will follow the

upward road today; I will keep my face to the light. I will think high thoughts as I go my way; I will do what I know is right. I will look for the flowers by the side of the road; I will laugh and love and be strong. I will try to lighten another's load this day as I fare along."

At one point, after being told that I was no longer permitted to see my grandchildren, I needed to make a change. I decided to spend time in upstate New York to be near my childhood friend, who loved and supported me. As it turned out, she needed quite a bit of help herself as a result of an accident, which I was able to provide for her. I gave her my time, energy, and love, even as I dealt with my own broken heart. It was good to focus on someone else, and looking back, I realize how much helping her helped me.

Mahatma Gandhi said, "The best way to find yourself is to lose yourself in the service of others." Devoting time and energy to others not only helps them, it helps us. For it is often in giving that we find our way back from sadness and grief.

> If you want happiness for an hour, take a nap.
> If you want happiness for a day, go fishing.
> If you want happiness for a year, inherit a fortune.
> If you want happiness for a lifetime, help someone else.
> —Chinese Proverb

48. Perceptions

> Men are disturbed not by the things that happen,
> but by their opinion of the things that happen.
> —Epictetus

It is often said that there are two sides to every story, and the truth lies somewhere in the middle. In many cases, it's difficult to establish absolute truth in a given situation because people have wildly divergent perceptions.

We humans experience events so differently, it's a wonder we agree on anything. For example, two people can listen to the same speech, one finding it poignant and relevant, the other finding it pedantic and boring. Each of us is unique. We have our own particular responses to and perceptions of shared circumstances, making it challenging to find common ground. We stubbornly cling to what we believe is the truth, as if our opinions and perspectives were indisputable. In the words of writer Anaïs Nin, "We don't see things as they are. We see them as we are."

Our adult children typically hold on tightly to their opinions of us, their parents. If they have an agenda that is unknown to us, we are caught off guard. We find ourselves confused as to how to repair the bridge between us before it collapses. If the bridge ultimately falls to pieces, it leaves us teetering, wondering what the hell happened.

You may have tried everything you could think of to keep the relationship with your adult child intact. You may have extended your hands to them, in the hopes of finding a middle ground, only to have them slapped away because of the gulf between your respective perceptions.

Everyone has their own impressions and opinions over which you have no control. But you do have control over your own.

When you start rehashing your heartbreaking story of alienation, missing your grandchildren or remembering harsh words and actions, catch yourself and stop. Remember that you're only *thinking*, that these are just *thoughts,* and you can choose to redirect them. You're not burying them, only changing them. Keep reminding yourself that you cannot change your adult child's perceptions, but you can change yours by letting go of any need you might have to make sense of their behaviors and opinions.

Comedian George Carlin described perception in this humorous way: "Some people see the cup as half-empty. Some people see the cup as half-full. I see the cup as too large."

Change all negative ideas you have about who you were in the past, and forgive yourself for any mistakes you made as a parent. Love and appreciate the person you are now.

> Reject your sense of injury and the injury itself disappears.
> —Marcus Aurelius

49. Everything Changes

Our lives are in a constant state of flux. By accepting the transient nature of all things, we set ourselves free, and life becomes deeply meaningful.

We are only renting space on this earth. Even though we're painfully aware that our time here will come to an end, we nevertheless spend our lives working to build security when there is none. We form relationships, get married, save money, buy homes, all in the interest of creating a reassuring solidity.

William Shakespeare wrote, "All the world's a stage, and all the men and women merely players." We make our entrances, play out our dramas and comedies, and ultimately make our exits. People come and go, the props change, the curtain rises and falls. "Life's but a walking shadow."

We search for ways to avoid uncertainty and change, but our existence is fundamentally built on shifting sands of impermanence. We cling to branches with the illusion of safety, all the while ignoring the fact that branches can snap at any time, sending us plummeting into an emotional abyss.

One day, the relationships with our estranged loved ones may mend; we have no way of knowing. But we do know that as life goes on, we will change, they will change, and the world around us will change.

By learning to view the unpredictability of life as an adventure, we can choose to let go of worry, abandon fear, and enjoy the ride.

We can learn to live in and appreciate the moment. There is an Australian Aboriginal saying: "We are all visitors to this time, this place. We are just passing through. We are here to observe, to learn, to grow, to love, and then we return home."

Recently, I was feeling down about the estrangement between my son and me, wondering when or if we will ever heal it. I became rather depressed and anxious about the swift passage of time, with no resolution in sight, when I brought myself back to the present. I stopped what I was doing and walked outside. I looked up at darkening clouds and watched autumn leaves skittering along the ground as a gusty wind rose up. Soon it began to rain, and I went back inside to the cozy warmth of my home. The problem didn't change, but by focusing on the present and rebooting my mind, I felt better.

By cultivating a state of awareness of the inevitability of change and the reality of impermanence, we develop an appreciation for the present and enjoy all the precious, vividly beautiful, ephemeral moments of each amazing day.

> If you realize that all things change, there is nothing you will try to hold on to.
>
> —Lao Tzu

50. Backsliding

> There is something you must always remember. You are braver that you believe, stronger than you seem, and smarter than you think.
> —Winnie the Pooh

You're getting better. Your grandchildren aren't foremost in your mind, and you feel happier, lighter. You're laughing more, enjoying food, seeing friends, and maybe even going on a weekend getaway.

But suddenly, when you least expect it, you get sucker-punched. Boom! Maybe you come across a card one of the kids made for you when they were little, or you see a picture of your grandchildren on social media. They all look so happy in the picture; how can this be? Is anyone thinking of you, the missing grandparent? You feel uncomfortably envious, because from all appearances, they are going on with their lives without you, while your own life is stalled, your heart turned inside out.

Just when you were coping well enough to find some enjoyment in your life without them, you backslide. And you wonder if you'll survive it this time.

Know that you will. Refuse to despair; refuse to be broken. You've climbed out of the quicksand of sadness before, and you can do it again. You have acquired new skills, and a new spiritual awareness is dawning within you. You may be powerless over the situation you're in, but you're *not* powerless over your own thoughts and attitudes.

Choose to brush yourself off and go forward on strong legs, with a warrior's heart beating in your chest. Because even without your grown child and grandchildren, your life is valuable and worth living to the fullest.

You are stronger and more courageous than you know.

> Fall seven times, stand up eight.
> —Japanese proverb.

51. Forgiving Yourself

> The unforgiving mind is full of fear, and offers love no room to be itself; no place where it can spread its wings in peace and soar above the turmoil of the world. The unforgiving mind is sad, without the hope of respite and release from pain. It suffers and abides in misery, peering about in darkness, seeing not, yet certain of the danger lurking there.
> —*A Course in Miracles*

Are there past mistakes you made, especially as a young parent, for which you feel remorse or regret? Did you miss a ballgame or a recital that was important to your young child? Were you an under- or overprotective parent? More recently, do you regret something you did or said in the heat of an argument? Do you wish you had behaved differently during the bewildering and distressing events that ultimately led to estrangement?

Forgive yourself for your shortcomings, past and present. Forgive yourself for being flawed. Let go of the torture of perfectionism. You did your best with what you knew at the time. It's that simple.

For too long, I carried a heavy weight of guilt and shame that affected me physically, mentally, and emotionally. One day, I realized that I needed to forgive myself for mistakes I'd made, and to be honest, I needed to look at my own stuff and begin healing on a deep level.

William Shakespeare wrote, "Do as the heavens have done, forget your evil; With them forgive yourself." If you choose to begin the process of forgiving yourself, you will have to muster up the courage to admit your imperfections and mistakes. It's not easy to admit where you have failed. It can be very painful to experience the sadness, shame, guilt, anger, or despair that may come up, but by processing these feelings, you will gain clarity and relief.

After getting in touch with your feelings about past errors in judgment, begin the process of absolution and self-forgiveness. Have compassion for yourself. When you do this, you'll feel freer and happier, and you'll more easily forgive everyone else, as well. If you have difficulty forgiving someone, find the part of yourself that you have not yet forgiven. You can only forgive others to the degree that you can forgive yourself.

> You cannot travel back in time to fix your mistakes, but you can learn from them and forgive yourself for not knowing better.
> —Leon Brown

52. Walking

> Take a walk outside–it will serve you far more than pacing around in your mind.
> —Rasheed Ogunlaru

There have been times when I obsessed so much about being estranged from my son and his family, I wondered if I was going crazy. It became clear that I needed to rise above the level of ruminating about what "he said, she said, and how could they?" and find healthy, viable ways to deal with the heartache I was experiencing.

Poets and philosophers have all stressed the importance of connecting with nature. By changing the focus from the many concerns of our lives—how we look, what we have, and what we do—to our spirit and essence, we restore our minds, hearts, and souls.

"I took a walk in the woods and came out taller than the trees," wrote Henry David Thoreau. When I go for a walk in nature, I'm quiet and, for a time, untroubled. As I hike under a canopy of pines or stroll along a shore, sand under my feet and saltwater around my ankles, I breathe in the fresh air, and my cares temporarily fall away.

Philosopher Søren Kierkegaard said, "Above all, do not lose your desire to walk. Every day I walk myself into a state of well-being and walk away from every illness. I have walked myself into my best thoughts, and I know of no thought so burdensome that one cannot walk away from it."

Although walking may not be a cure-all for the sad circumstances of alienation and estrangement, it is a wonderful, healthy way to distance yourself from your problems. So take a walk in a park or go for a hike in the woods, and rejuvenate yourself. Walk in the rain, let wind blow your hair back, stand beneath a quiet snowfall, and catch snowflakes on your tongue. Any experience of the beauty of the natural world will connect you with your own true nature.

> I wonder if the snow loves the trees and fields, that it kisses them so gently? And then it covers them up snug, you know, with a white quilt; and perhaps it says, "Go to sleep, darlings, till the summer comes again."
>
> —Lewis Carroll

53. The Problem with Comparisons

One of the most harmful things we can do to ourselves is to compare our circumstances to someone else's. When you make comparisons, someone wins and someone loses. In the words of author Jack Canfield, "I generally find that comparison is the fast track to unhappiness. No one ever compares themselves to someone else and comes out even. Nine times out of ten, we compare ourselves to people who are somehow better than us and end up feeling more inadequate."

Let's face it: it's difficult to witness other grandparents enjoying their grandchildren when we have been deprived of ours. Being disrespected by our adult child and cheated out of a normal relationship with our grandchildren makes it tempting to fall into the trap of comparing our situation to one that's ideal. In addition, it's challenging to live in a society where the family is idealized and having grandchildren is depicted as one of the greatest joys in life. When we have lost contact with our own grandchildren, this social construct can be very upsetting.

In most cases of estrangement, the heartbreak never leaves, and we drag it around like an uncomfortable appendage. But as with everything, there is an upside and a downside. The downside is that, at times, we may feel emotionally exhausted and too weak to carry this burden; the upside is that we grow stronger, even as scar tissue grows around our broken hearts.

Many baby boomers are now grandparents, and films,

TV shows, commercials, and books about grandparenting are ubiquitous. There is considerable attention on the subject of grandparents aging-in-place, with family members advocating for them and loving them. It's difficult, though, to see and hear such magical interpretations of grandparenting when we have been robbed of it altogether

Life isn't always fair or logical. As sad as it is to be cut off from your grandchildren, there may be aspects of your life that, when compared to grandparents who *do* have access to their grandchildren, might be enviable. For example, I'm reminded of a friend of mine who has three grown children, one of whom she has been estranged from for several years. Happily, she is able to pour her love into her other grown kids and grandchildren, which is a significant compensation, but for the moment, she's unemployed and has some health issues. I have no other grandkids to shower my love upon, but I am blessed with a beautiful home, good friends, and good health. It's futile to compare ourselves and our situations to anyone because we all have challenges.

As a grandparent without your grandchildren, you have a choice: You can stay at home and control your stimuli, or you can step out into the world, knowing full well that you will encounter other grandparents with their grandchildren. You can choose to participate in this happy crowd of intact families and forget for a while your own sadness and deprivation by refusing to compare your situation to theirs. You can choose to be glad for these families simply because you make room in your heart to do so.

French author and Nobel laureate André Gide wrote, "In order to be utterly happy the only thing necessary is to refrain from comparing." It's fruitless and punishing to compare your circumstances to others. You have your own story, your own destiny, your own joys, and your own sorrows. Celebrate your life and celebrate the lives of others. Be generous, for by giving to others and stepping outside of yourself, you find a higher purpose and the sweetest grace.

> Love asks no questions. Its natural state is one of extension and expansion, not comparison and measurement.
>
> —Gerald Jampolsky

54. Codependency

Estrangement is particularly hard on parents and grandparents who are overly attached to their adult child and grandchildren. Unfortunately, many of our relationships with our children are cloaked in our own codependency. Our feelings are hurt when they don't call; we find ourselves wanting them to approve of us, which creates expectations, anxiety, and disappointment. We may have begun to feel that our desire to have a relationship with them is one-sided because we are doing most, if not all, of the work. Finally, if we fear that our relationship is in jeopardy, our behavior may devolve into people-pleasing, walking on eggshells, or deferring to our adult child's unreasonable demands in order to stay in the family.

Many of us are codependent, which causes the relationships with our kids to be based on need rather than healthy mutual respect. When estrangement occurs, we are unable to digest the fact that we have been disrespected and abandoned by them. We tend to feel guilty, hurt, shamed, and angry, and we lose trust in ourselves. We say yes when we want to say no. We overanalyze and obsess about what we might have done wrong or could have done better. In other words, we beat ourselves up.

This may be difficult to accept, but the truth is this: We don't need our kids; we just *want* them too much. It's heartbreaking to be estranged, and some days, we feel we can't go on. But if we can learn to accept that it's possible to live without them, we can find some peace.

Estrangement is particularly hard on parents and grandparents who turned themselves inside out to stay solvent in a system that emotionally bankrupted them. They can't bear what happened; they feel like they might die without their loved ones. And, sadly, there have been a number of suicides committed by parents and grandparents who have been estranged.

Melody Beattie, an expert on codependency, says, "The formula is simple: In any given situation, detach and ask, 'What do I need to do to take care of myself?'" Start by being gentle, kind, and loving to yourself. Relax. Do the work necessary to change your thinking and perceptions. Take a personal inventory, and identify your weak spots. For example, does your happiness depend on a call from your adult child? Do you take things too personally? Have you told lies to make yourself more acceptable or likable? It will take time, but you can learn to release what is hindering you from moving forward, such as overattachment to your adult child, low self-esteem, or fear of being alone.

Happiness is a choice. I know how tough it is, but you can choose to be happy—and *be* happy—even without the presence of your adult child and grandchildren.

> Today I will stop trying to control my relationships. I will participate at a reasonable level and let the other person do the same. I can let go, knowing that the relationship will find its own life—or not—and that I don't have to do all the work, only my share.
> —Melody Beattie

55. Detachment

> There will be an answer, let it be.
> —The Beatles

One day, following heart-wrenching events leading to estrangement from my son and his family, I was driving on Pacific Coast Highway in California when the song "Let It Be" came on the radio. Even though I'd heard this song countless times, I was nevertheless struck by the relevance of the lyrics. I made a decision that detachment and learning to "let it be" would be how the way to navigate the sorrows I was experiencing.

What is detachment? Detachment is separating oneself from a person, group, or situation. It is being unattached to outcome. Detachment requires dedication to living in a state of awareness, consciousness, and nonresistance. It requires facing reality and letting go when you recognize that you are powerless to change someone else's behavior. It requires calling on a higher power, whether it be the God of your understanding or your own higher self, to help you process and release any fears and beliefs that no longer serve you. It requires strengthening your heart and mind by relaxing your grip on what you think you need to hold onto and letting it gently drop away.

Detachment gives you the freedom to be who you are without concerning yourself with what others think of you. As you learn detachment, you find it unacceptable to tiptoe around others in order to either gain their approval or avoid disapproval. You set your own boundaries, and you respect the boundaries of others. You are no one's slave; you're not tethered to any rules but those by which you choose to live. You dance your own beautiful dance, no matter what anyone thinks of your style or footwork.

You no longer waste time and energy judging, comparing, or forming opinions of others. You understand that the behaviors of others define *them*, not you. If anyone has been unkind to you, there is a good chance it's because they are ignorant, unhappy or suffering. Knowing this, you bless them and turn your attention to your own life, your own needs, your own creativity and joy.

The more you emotionally disengage from your adult child and grandchildren, the happier you will become. Your focus shifts from obsessing about where they are, what they're doing or whether you will ever see them again to accepting any and all possibilities. You come back to the moment. Even though it may be difficult, you detach, compassionately and lovingly, as you embrace your own precious life.

> Release and detach from every person, every circumstance, every condition, and every situation that no longer serves a divine purpose in your life. All things have a season, and all seasons must come to an end. Choose a new season, filled with purposeful thoughts and activities.
> —Iyanla Vanzant

56. Making Amends

> The most important trip you may take in life is meeting people halfway.
> —Henry Boye

Everyone makes mistakes from time to time. Everyone says the wrong thing, asks the wrong question, makes a false assumption. We're human and, therefore, imperfect beings.

Reasonable people reflect on their own behavior and, when appropriate, take responsibility for it, which includes apologizing and making amends to someone they have hurt or angered. In turn, reasonable people are receptive to an apology.

Have you done anything that might require an apology? Do you think it might be worth reflecting on your own behavior and how it may (or may not) have contributed to the estrangement and alienation you're experiencing?

We often resist apologizing to those who have hurt and abused us, which is understandable. As dishonored parents and grandparents, we think it more appropriate that our estranged adult children apologize to *us*. After all, they expelled us from their family and cut us off from our grandchildren. However, it can't hurt to reach out to your adult child, if possible, listen with an open heart, and strive to understand her or his point of view. In the end, you can decide to offer apologies or not.

Your only responsibility is to take care of your side of the fence. What they do with their side is up to them.

As the parent and elder, you have hopefully acquired a good amount of wisdom by now. You were once as young as your grown child is now and can remember what it was like and all the things you hadn't learned yet. As the wise person you've become, you can afford to be generous, open, and compassionate.

Unfortunately, some circumstances are almost impossible to navigate, where the reasons or motivations for your alienator's actions are never made clear, perhaps to deliberately avoid the possibility of a viable solution. Even your best efforts will be ineffective if the other party isn't interested in reconciliation or healing.

If you have decided that an apology from you is in order, offer one. People who are fair, compassionate, and forgiving will accept your apology. If not, take comfort in the fact that you reached out with loving intentions and did your best to heal the relationship. That's all you can do.

> Have a heart that never hardens, and a temper that never tires, and a touch that never hurts.
> —Charles Dickens

57. Coulda, Shoulda, Woulda

We parents and grandparents have a tough time letting go. Even in the face of indisputable evidence that our adult children have let go of *us*, we soldier on, doing all we can to mend our relationships with them.

We ask ourselves what we could have done differently, what we should have said, or what would have happened if we'd tried a different tact. But by continually revisiting and belaboring memories of the difficult events of alienation, we only torture ourselves. Harping on what we could have, should have, or would have done results in frustration and misery. The fact is, we said what we said and did what we did; we made choices that seemed appropriate at the time. And even if we made mistakes, that was then, and now it's time to make peace with it all.

Basketball coach Pat Riley said, "There's no such thing as coulda, shoulda, or woulda. If you shoulda and coulda, you woulda done it." It is masochistic to go over and over the past; like riding a stationary bicycle, we go nowhere and only exhaust ourselves. Indulging in feelings of regret, guilt, or rejection is futile. We can't change what happened, and we can't change what's in our grown child's mind. We did our best with what we knew at the time, and that is all that can be asked of us.

There are still nights when I toss and turn, my thoughts going around in circles. I find myself re-examining decisions made, reviewing things said (and unsaid), and replaying the past in my head. Eventually, I realize that it's all pointless, and I stop, breathe deeply, and say a prayer to God, angels, elves, or whoever is listening to us here on earth, that goes more or less like this: "Help me change my thoughts from past regrets and give me the strength to do what's best for my health and happiness now. Show me how to be more loving toward myself and others. Enlighten me as to what I am on this earth to do."

If you experience sleepless nights because of out-of-control obsessing about your problems, it can help to say a prayer or affirmation, or just imagine something pleasant, like walking on a beautiful beach. The act of redirecting your thoughts will reset your brain and give you much-needed relief from worry and rumination.

> Free yourself from the burden of a past you cannot change.
> —Dr. Steve Maraboli

58. Tough Love

> Make us to choose the harder right instead of the easier wrong, and never to be content with a half truth when the whole can be won.
> —West Point Cadet Prayer

Tough love means being concerned about a person's welfare, especially that of an addict or a child, by requiring them to take responsibility for their actions. While it's based in compassion, it is unsentimental.

It may be time to practice some tough love on yourself.

I reached a point in my healing and recovery when it felt like my thoughts were out of control. Millions of thoughts whirled around in my head, and before I knew it, I was a nervous wreck. I knew I had to make some significant changes in order to have any quality of life. I started experimenting with being aware of thoughts that popped into my head. If they were constructive thoughts, I would embrace them; if they were negative or destructive, I'd challenge them and dismiss them. For example, if I felt good about a job I'd done, I'd let myself be happy about it. If I told myself something negative, like believing I was alone in the world, I would remind myself that I'm not alone and that I have plenty of people who care about me.

If you're having a problem with addictive thought processes, such as ruminating about your alienators or constantly reviewing the events leading up to estrangement, you might need to set some thought boundaries. Start watching your thought patterns, and if you become aware of those that perpetuate the sadness and frustration of your situation, intercept them and replace them with uplifting, affirming thoughts. Make a shift from addictive thinking to recovery thinking, choosing thoughts that support your health and happiness. As the saying goes, "You don't drown by falling in the water. You drown by staying there."

Since you can't force your adult children to take responsibility for their actions, the only thing you can do is take responsibility for yours. Practice self-discipline, self-reflection, and self-love. Love yourself enough to face the many challenges in your life because, ultimately, that's what will heal you.

Face the truth in all things. Choose the harder right rather than the easier wrong. Be tough on self-defeating thought habits and control them, rather than letting them control you.

> If you're gonna make a change, you're gonna have to operate from a new belief that says life happens not *to* me but *for* me.
> —Tony Robbins

59. The Worry Habit

> Real difficulties can be overcome, it is only the imaginary ones that are unconquerable.
> —Theodore N. Vail

When we feel that life is out of control, we often worry and fret. Unfortunately, worry puts our bodies, minds, and emotions under a lot of stress. And the more we worry, the more we seem to attract what we *don't* want.

As alienated grandparents, we worry that we are missing the bonding years with our grandkids; we worry that the relationship we once had with our adult child is forever damaged; we worry that the estrangement will never resolve and we'll grow old alone.

But what's the point of worrying? Worry will not only make you more depressed and anxious, it can jeopardize your health. Excessive worry can cause headaches, upset stomach, high blood pressure, and poor sleep due to spikes in cortisol and adrenal depletion. There is no upside to worry.

Instead of agonizing over the unknowable future, visualize a happy outcome and calmly bring yourself back the fullness of the present moment. Make a cup of tea, gaze out the window at the sky, or write your thoughts and feelings in a journal. Consciously redirect your mind to brighter, more positive thoughts.

Worry can be all-consuming, eroding your vitality and depleting your energy. It's just not worth it. So take a chill pill. Don't worry, be happy. (Seriously.) Your body, mind, and spirit will thank you for it.

> If a problem is fixable, if a situation is such that you can do something about it, then there is no need to worry. If it's not fixable, then there is no help in worrying. There is no benefit in worrying whatsoever.
> —His Holiness, the Dalai Lama XIV

60. Detoxing

I was watching a show recently about the importance of detoxing periodically to cleanse the body of toxins that have built up due to improper diet, pollution, or lack of exercise. Detoxing is good for energy, mood, and weight loss, and it reduces inflammation. I started to think about the benefits of this practice, especially as it relates to estrangement.

Taking it a bit further than just physical detoxing, in which you abstain from certain substances, like sugar and junk food, how about detoxing from habitual negative and obsessive thoughts, self-sabotaging behaviors, constant self-doubt, and debilitating sadness? That would also include limiting or discontinuing contact with people who are negative, critical, and judgmental, with whom we may have unhealthy relationships.

Our relationship with our adult children may be toxic at this time. If they are angry, blaming, unreasonable, unkind, and only interested in pointing their fingers in our direction, it's impossible to have a healthy relationship with them.

As a result of being treated with such injurious disrespect by our grown children, we ourselves become emotionally and mentally toxic. We become hypervigilant, constantly scanning our surroundings to find ways to stay safe in a precarious family dynamic. We, the parents, do most, if not all, of the compromising. We become upset, anxious, and fearful that if we don't conform to our adult children's demands, we'll be expelled from the family. This creates an unwholesome environment in our minds, our emotions, and our bodies.

It may be time for a mental and emotional detox.

If your thoughts are habitually stuck in a negative loop, stop and figure out what you want and need to change. Write down your weaknesses and strengths. Figure out how to use your strengths—like honesty, compassion, integrity, patience, open-mindedness, or humor—to overcome obstacles to peace and happiness, such as worry, fear, denial, or resistance to change. Understand that this will take work and time, and there will be temporary setbacks. It's okay to cry when you need to, and it's okay to feel discouraged at times. Just keep moving forward and ridding yourself of self-defeating thoughts by taking action for your health and well-being. For example, if you fall off the wagon and start ruminating about your adult child, forgive yourself and reinforce your desire to be happy. In addition, you may choose to face the possibility that it would best to rid yourself of the need to have a relationship with your child, at least for now, until there is a mutual willingness to reconnect and reconcile.

Author John C. Maxwell said, "If we're growing, we are always going to be out of our comfort zone." It's tough to detoxify our thoughts and feelings. Like the initial discomfort that often occurs when starting a physical detox, you might, in the beginning, feel uncomfortable as you get rid of all the junk in your emotional body. Lots of feelings will come up. You may feel disoriented for a while, sick at heart, and overwhelmed, but if you stick with it and continue to be your own advocate for peace, health, and happiness, your mind will clear, and your strength and enthusiasm will improve. Making positive changes is courageous and empowering.

> You don't ever have to feel guilty about removing toxic people from your life. It doesn't matter whether someone is a relative, romantic interest, employer, childhood friend or a new acquaintance—you don't

have to make room for people who cause you pain or make you feel small. It's one thing if a person owns up to their behavior and makes an effort to change. But if a person disregards your feelings, ignores your boundaries, and continues to treat you in a harmful way, they need to go.

—Daniell Koepke

61. Healthy Relationships

Whenever two people are in a relationship of any kind, conflicts and disappointments are inevitable. There is much to learn within a relationship, but we often resist the lessons. Our egos get in the way. We want to be right, to be in control, and to feel invulnerable. Unfortunately, these are not achievable goals (or even worthy ones).

Everyone has been hurt. Everyone has childhood wounds and emotional scars. We have all been treated unkindly at times. We walk through relationships, whether with a friend, a family member, a partner, or a spouse, wanting to love and to be loved. Inevitably, we experience stress and may become frustrated, critical, needy, or angry, often without any insights as to the genesis of these feelings and behaviors. Wayne Dyer said, "Problems in relationships occur because each person is concentrating on what is missing in the other person." In many relationships, our wounds bump into each other in a miserable dance of neuroses that we don't understand, let alone know how to heal.

So what does a *healthy* relationship look like?

Ideally, whether it's a relationship with a partner, an adult child, a relative, or a friend, we create a conscious, safe place to be and to grow. We tacitly agree to support each other's evolution in a loving way, basing the relationship on mutual respect, compassion, and trust. We commit to owning our personal wounds, supporting each other as we work through them and forgiving each other. We cry, we laugh, we learn, we heal. A healthy relationship exists in light and spreads outward from its core of love.

Over the years of being estranged from my son and daughter-in-law, my self-esteem crumbled. My life was so negatively impacted by the tragedy of losing these relationships that I struggled with feelings of unworthiness. As a result, I stayed too long in other unhealthy relationships. When I became aware of this, I took an honest look at those relationships, and I ended several friendships that were not in my best interest to continue. By letting go, I felt lighter because I honored my need for more conscious relationships.

Is there anyone in your life who is a crazy-maker, who sucks your energy, who is unkind, is inconsiderate, and undermines you? Are any of your relationships one-sided, with you doing most of the work? Has someone lied to you on more than one occasion? Do you feel uncomfortable being vulnerable and authentic in the company of that person? Have you been holding onto a relationship out of fear or overdependence?

If you decide to take an honest look at your relationships, including the one you once had with your adult child, you will experience myriad emotions. You may feel sad that one or more of your relationships isn't working out; you may fear the unknown and possible future loneliness if you decide to leave it. But why stay in a relationship that doesn't validate you?

By honoring your desire for a mutually satisfying relationship based on respect, trust, and support, you are choosing the path of love: love for yourself and love for another. It's a tough process, and it takes courage to admit that a relationship may no longer be viable. By working at having healthy, loving relationships, you increase your chances of improving your current ones and enjoying healthier relationships in the future.

> Nothing is perfect. Life is messy. Relationships are complex. Outcomes are uncertain. People are irrational.
> —Hugh Mackay

62. Believing You're Good Enough

> And above all things, never think that you're not good enough yourself. A man should never think that. My belief is that in life people will take you at your own reckoning.
> —Isaac Asimov

If you've been working on healing from alienation and estrangement, you have probably asked yourself these questions: How do I go on? What do I believe, want, hope for? How will I find happiness again? How can I live without my adult child and grandchildren?

Life gives us lesson upon lesson upon lesson. We never seem to arrive at the ultimate answer. We repeat our mistakes, stalling our growth because of fear, denial, or lack of awareness. We keep bumping into walls until we learn to cut a pathway through them or go around them. We don't want to feel pain and will do anything to escape it, even avoiding the truth, which ultimately causes more pain. But pain is inevitable if we're going to evolve and grow into the fullness of who we truly are.

When we were young, many of us learned that we needed approval from others. Miguel Ruiz writes, "Just being ourselves is the biggest fear of humans. We have learned to live our lives trying to satisfy other people's demands. We have learned to live by other people's points of view because of the fear of not being accepted and of not being good enough for someone else."

We must believe that we are whole and good, just as we are. Once we understand this, it won't matter if people don't like us, because we like ourselves. We will no longer believe that we were cut off from our family because we're not good enough. Behavioral scientist Steve Marabolli observes, "There are some people who will never see you as being good enough. That is their shortcoming, not yours."

As we grow and evolve, our sadness turns to joy as we learn to live in the light of our true spirit. One morning we wake up and finally, truly, believe that we are good enough and worthy of love.

> It's a lie to think you're not good enough. It's a lie to think you're not worth anything.
> —Nick Vujicic

63. Higher Ground

> You yourself are your own obstacle, rise above yourself.
>
> —Hafiz

It's not easy to be disrespected by your grown child. It's normal to feel anger, indignation and hurt in the face of such disregard.

Your adult child or a gatekeeper may have accused you of transgressions, real or imagined, and you felt defensive and bewildered. At some point, communication may have spun out of control, and no one knew what to do next. It seemed that it would take a mediator sent from heaven to find neutral ground in the midst of so much confusion and conflict.

Whether you still have some contact with your adult child or have been completely estranged, it's never too late to search for a higher ground. For example, you can learn to be more patient, more allowing. You can work on your attitudes, your thought patterns, and any anger or resentment you may be holding onto. And you can set healthier boundaries.

Instead of waiting for an apology, let it go. Instead of brooding about the past or fretting about the future, let it go. Your grown child may have unmet needs that are driving their anger. Gain some perspective about your adult child's predicament, understand their struggles, and have compassion for their choices.

Although I still carry the weight of mistakes I made with my son and problems they may have caused him in his life, I decided that after years of frustration and misunderstandings, the healthiest option was to disentangle myself. I still love him, always will, and I deeply mourn the loss of our relationship, but I need to rise above the craziness and find some peace. Spiritual teacher Marianne Williamson writes:

> Always seek less turbulent skies.
> Hurt. Fly above it.
> Betrayal. Fly above it.
> Anger. Fly above it.
> You are the one who is flying the plane.

Most importantly, practice loving kindness, to yourself and to all living things. Love is the best place to dwell and to rest, and it's a sure way to serenity and peace.

64. Planning Ahead

> We cannot banish dangers, but we can banish fears.
> —David Sarnoff

As we age, many of us fear that we will become lonely, helpless, or irrelevant. We hear about elders who are moved to facilities, spending the rest of their lives in rumpled old clothes, staring blankly into space. They are at the mercy of caregivers who may or may not be skilled, compassionate, or aware of what's best for them. We worry that we'll wind up like those poor souls, with no advocates or adult children lovingly present in our lives.

These are real concerns and worthy of our attention. It would be smart to plan ahead and create some strategies for aging. This is not a pleasant subject; I get it. But if you ignore this factor of estrangement, you could wind up with an unpleasant predicament on your hands, like a sudden fall, a fracture, or a debilitating illness.

Winston Churchill said, "Let our advance worrying become advance thinking and planning." You can prepare for your older years in a way that will offer some comfort. For instance, if you can't rely on your grown child and have no partner or spouse, find someone who will agree to be your advocate and act on your behalf if the need should arise. Ask them to be your go-to person in the case of illness or an emergency. Discuss your preferences (e.g., whether you want a DNR [Do Not Resuscitate] order), and create a contingency plan for recovery and recuperation. Have a long-term plan for how and where you want to live as you age, make out a living will, and see that all your documents are in order, such as your last will and testament and instructions for your interment. Find and join a community that offers friendship and support for challenges similar to those you are facing. Reach out and help others as you help yourself.

What does it mean to you to grow older? Were you taught as a child that old age is something to be dreaded? Do you feel revulsion when around old people? Our society certainly doesn't support aging, and if you watch enough TV, you'll want to go hide in a closet with every new gray hair or wrinkle you acquire. Learn to change your thinking about aging and catch yourself when you have a negative thought about being old. Ask yourself where your opinions of old age originated and reject them if they are negative. Learn to embrace aging; why not? You've got nothing to lose by having a vision of yourself as healthy and vibrant as you age.

After you've made the necessary arrangements, you can relax and enjoy the freedom and peace of mind that comes from having a viable plan for what may lie ahead.

> In my youth I stressed freedom, and in my old age I stress order. I have made the great discovery that liberty is a product of order.
> —Will Durant

65. Choices

> May your choices reflect your hopes, not your fears.
> —Nelson Mandela

We often base our self-esteem on how others regard us. If we are treated well, we feel loved; if we are treated badly, we feel unloved. We have great difficulty in loving ourselves when we allow the judgments of others to define us.

Many parents and grandparents become physically ill, some with life-threatening conditions, after being alienated and estranged from their adult child and grandchildren. The stress, devastation, and heartbreak of losing a relationship with loved ones is not to be taken lightly; it can lead to serious illnesses and even death.

If we continue to give our grown children power over our health and well-being, we will never have a moment's peace. We must not internalize any negative opinions they may have of us because they are perceiving us through their own filters and notions. Instead, we must empower ourselves by getting rid of guilt, shame, and negative self-worth and, instead, cultivating confidence, self-respect, and loving acceptance.

Once we understand that unless we choose to love ourselves by turning the locus of control from outside ourselves to within, we will never stop looking for approval and love.

We can choose to turn away from the dysfunction of others. We can choose to take care of ourselves and heal our bodies, minds, and hearts. We can create happiness and peace for ourselves.

In the words of author Carolyn Myss, "Always go with the choice that scares you the most, because that's the one that is going to require the most from you."

The quality of our lives rests on the choices we make, how we perceive events, and what we allow in our consciousness. Today, we can choose to embrace our challenges because they propel us to learn and to grow by searching for the gifts within the trials. We can choose to appreciate our own heartfelt efforts to love ourselves unconditionally and extend that love to others. And we can choose to acknowledge all that is bright, blessed, and beautiful.

> Your destiny is to fulfill those things upon which you focus most intently. So choose to keep your focus on that which is truly magnificent, beautiful, uplifting and joyful. Your life is always moving toward something.
>
> —Ralph Marston

66. Christmas

> Some say that ever 'gainst that season comes
> Whereon our Savior's birth is celebrated,
> The bird of dawning singeth all night long.
> And then, they say, no spirit dare abroad,
> The nights are wholesome, then no planets strike,
> No fairy takes nor witch hath power to charm,
> So hallowed and so gracious is the time.
> —William Shakespeare, *Hamlet*

Christmas is a magical season. Trees are decorated, the crisp smell of evergreen permeates the air, fires warm us. We hear familiar carols playing, plan holiday dinners, buy gifts for loved ones, and have hope in our hearts for good times and loving connections.

For those of us who are estranged from our adult child and missing our grandchildren, the holidays are a huge challenge. It is a time when our brain chemistry is on high alert. We are at risk for depression, even illness, and our bodies, minds, and hearts are severely compromised. The holidays were designed to be a time of celebrating with family, yet how do we have ourselves a merry little Christmas without them?

There were many holidays when I was so sad and depressed, I cried on and off for the entire day. Being rejected by my child felt unbearable, and I had no choice but to bear it. My heart ached, and I could find no relief. I felt an existential terror that I was stuck in a life that would be forever affected by estrangement. I had a difficult time not only getting through the day but finding ways to cope. With each passing year, however, I learned effective ways of managing the stress and sadness. For example, I use turnaround thoughts, practice gratitude and acceptance, and trust that my life has a reason for being. I take a time-out from the busy day and meditate for a few minutes or just rest. I use compartmentalization and change my focus from thinking about what I am missing to appreciating what is happening in the moment.

We must make a conscious decision to enjoy the day and spend it in the company of people who love and respect us. We must decide to be happy anyway. Let's tap into the childlike wonder we once felt during the Christmas season and allow ourselves some fun, laughter, and merriment.

As the holidays approach, we see our friends enjoying visits from their children and grandchildren. Their homes are full of several generations of family, yummy smells waft from the kitchen, and gifts are joyously exchanged. Although it's difficult to witness others enjoying what we cannot have, it's best to share in their good fortune and be happy for them. Celebrate what we *do* have and be joyful, as much as possible

While Christmas lights twinkle all around, let the light within you twinkle and shine over the mantle of your own loving heart. You have lifted yourself up. You are alive and well, and that is the greatest victory, the greatest gift of all.

67. Integrity

A person with integrity is said to be one who faces the truth, speaks the truth and stands firm in the truth.

For any relationship to be successful, there has to be honest communication and compromise. But we fall short of that ideal if we are too emotionally dependent on others or fear the loss of their love and affection. In the case of a potential alienation, we often abandon our own truth by agreeing with our adult child or a gatekeeper in order to keep the peace, thereby allowing ourselves to be manipulated in ways that are detrimental to our mental and emotional health. As a result, we wind up adapting our behaviors to survive in an unhealthy psychological dynamic.

For example, many of us parents and grandparents tiptoe around land mine issues with our adult children or their spouse. Over time, we come to the unhappy realization that we no longer have a voice in these relationships and continually swallow our anger, hurt, and frustration. We do whatever we can to prevent the unthinkable, which is being cut off from our precious grandchildren. But by complying with unreasonable demands issued by our alienators, our loss is compounded if it doesn't work out, because we lose not only our grandchildren but our self-respect.

William Shakespeare wrote, "To thine own self be true, and it must follow, as the night the day, thou canst not then be false to any man." If you have maintained an open mind, considered creative compromises whenever possible, and stood in loving compassion and honesty throughout the events leading to estrangement, you have done all you can. There isn't always a clear answer or solution. In the words of Sigmund Freud, "Sometimes a cigar is just a cigar," and at some point, you recognize that the outcome you had hoped for may not come to fruition. If your adult child has built a fence, it's not your job to tear it down. The situation is what it is, and in order to maintain your dignity, sanity, health, and integrity, you learn to accept the unacceptable. You recognize that it's best to go on with life because you can't change, control, or cure your child, only yourself. And though you continue to live as full a life as possible without your loved ones, your door is always open for reconciliation.

It takes courage to admit the truth. It takes courage to face the reality of estrangement. It takes courage to do the right thing, no matter how much it scares you. But if you come from a place of integrity, you'll be able to live with your choices, which will help make it all more bearable.

In the end, trust yourself and be true to yourself. That's the bottom line.

> To be nobody but yourself in a world which is doing its best, night and day, to make you everybody else means to fight the hardest battle which any human being can fight; and never stop fighting.
> —e.e. cummings

68. Taking Care of Yourself

Estranged parents and grandparents experience a wide range of emotions, from anger, rage, and shock to hurt, sadness, and despair. It's an emotional roller-coaster ride from hell.

In the midst of so much angst, it is imperative that you take care of yourself. You have experienced a trauma. You've lost your way. At times, you may not remember to eat, and normal sleep patterns are often disrupted. You may have vivid dreams about your adult child and your grandchildren; you may cry until your heart feels like it's torn to shreds. You may become absentminded, forget when you last took a shower, or when you had a day without tears.

It can be intense, to say the least.

When you have cried enough tears, missed enough meals, lost enough sleep, you will make a shift. You will become tired of the pathology and dysfunction that have been riding roughshod over your heart lately, and you'll make a healthy choice for yourself.

You will reclaim your life.

Start by being gentle with yourself. Take naps and warm baths. Get some body work, like massage or chiropractic. Take a class that interests you. Read inspirational books, sign up for a workshop, or take an educational webinar. Hang out with kindred spirits. Laugh. Turn on music and dance around the kitchen while you prepare a healthy meal. Go for a hike, and enjoy open spaces and fresh air. Breathe deeply. Stretch. Quiet your mind.

There's a whole wide world out there that doesn't include our adult child and grandkids. I have learned that I can enjoy my life despite missing the grandchildren I love and adore. I still feel sad at times, of course, but when I do, I deliberately and mindfully compartmentalize. To accomplish this, I sit quietly, breathing deeply and letting myself feel my emotions for a few minutes. Then I direct my attention to other matters. I visit with friends, take a brisk walk, watch a movie, take a dance class, or play with my dog. And although it seems that I can't completely escape the heartache of missing the children, I *can* consciously choose to derive some joy in life and carry on.

Writer Nora Roberts says it well: "If you don't go after what you want, you'll never have it. If you don't ask, the answer is always no. If you don't step forward, you're always in the same place." By making the courageous decision to step forward and live a full-hearted, happy, and healthy life, you will find meaning again.

> Love yourself first, and everything else falls in line. You really have to love yourself to get anything done in this world.
>
> —Lucille Ball

69. Solitude

Dealing with alienation and estrangement is a daily challenge: How to cope with the pain, how to live a normal life again, how to find any peace. Well-meaning friends may suggest that you keep busy, structure your time, and get out more. These are all good suggestions, and there is certainly a time for social activity and involvement.

There is also a time for solitude.

There were days I spent alone when I felt lost, raw, and vulnerable, just me and my troubled soul. I didn't know where to turn, who I was anymore, or how to stop the pain that pierced my heart. I cried many tears during those times of solitude, and miraculously, every tear I shed seemed to bring me closer to what Pope John Paul II called an "interior purification, silence, waiting."

We live in a society that is externally focused, caught up in quick fixes, shallow encounters, and instant experiences. We want immediate gratification and are often impatient with ongoing internal processes like anger, grief, or sadness. But when our hearts have been broken, it's difficult to just leap back into the flow of life because, for a time, we need the protective, womblike comfort of drawn curtains and soft shadows.

It is an act of courage to embrace solitude. By doing so, you access a part of your mind, your heart, and your soul that has been whispering to you, trying to get your attention. Rainer Maria Rilke wrote, "Go into yourself and see how deep the place is from which your life flows." As you surrender to an afternoon, a day, or a season alone, you become more intimately acquainted with who you really are, with all your perfect imperfections. As you turn inward, you face your demons and embrace your goodness, and the mask you've been wearing for so long slowly melts away, revealing your true and stunning beauty.

> Whosoever is delighted in solitude is either a wild beast or a god.
> —Aristotle

70. Changing Your Story

> You must have control of the authorship of your own destiny. The pen that writes your life story must be held in your own hand.
> —Irene C. Kassorla

Most of us get caught up in the stories of our lives. At this point, a big part of our story is about being alienated or ghosted by our adult children. We're devastated because they no longer call us or return our calls or texts; we feel shunned; we miss our grandchildren so much, it's almost a physical pain. We spend an enormous amount of time feeling emotionally wrecked, but at some point, when we get fed up with struggling, we decide to make some serious changes.

Author Alan Cohen describes it this way:

> It takes a lot of courage to release the familiar and seemingly secure, to embrace the new. But there is no real security in what is no longer meaningful. There is more security in the adventurous and exciting, for in movement there is life, and in change there is power.

For years, I felt envious of people who had functional, loving families; I resented those who had hurt me. I was stuck in wanting what I couldn't have and made myself miserable. I was defensive, was afraid of being hurt, and was often angry when I didn't even know why. I hated my life. Finally, I realized that I had to escape the shackles of old mind-sets, outdated expectations, tired perspectives, and negative paradigms. Kahil Gibran spoke of finding freedom by discarding "fragments of your own self." I had wasted too many years hoping that my son and I would reconcile and I would reunite with my grandchildren. One day, I realized that it was time to let go of my old story and create a new one.

Jungian psychologist Carl Greer wrote, "There is a possibly apocryphal story that in Southeast Asia, people catch monkeys by placing a banana in a box with a hole in the bottom and hanging the box from a tree. The monkey reaches in and grabs the banana but is unable to withdraw its hand. The clenched fist holding the banana is too big to fit through the hole. To escape, all the monkey has to do is release the banana. Sometimes, the monkeys hold on for a long time and are then captured. People, too, often give up their freedom by holding on to things too long."

What have you been telling yourself about being abandoned and estranged? Do you find yourself stuck in patterns of thoughts and behaviors that are counterproductive and harmful to your health and happiness? Are you sliding down a slippery slope of relentless rumination and depression until you can think of nothing but the circumstances of your estrangement?

Most of us resist acknowledging the parts of our lives that are painful. Maybe we feel shame, or we're embarrassed to admit, even to ourselves, that we made mistakes. At times, we may feel like our minds and emotions are running us, and we wonder how to free ourselves from the insanity of holding on to what isn't working. When we relive our old stories, we stay stuck in them. We make excuses for our behaviors, beliefs, and attitudes by blaming past events or other people. By doing this, we prolong the pain and stunt our own growth.

We are more than our past: our parents, kids, childhoods, jobs, marriages, partnerships, successes, and failures. It's time to explore the mystery of who we are and reclaim our self-respect, power, and nobility.

If you want to change your story, you must have courage and a strong desire to let go of habits that are keeping you chained to your painful old story and form new habits that create health and fulfillment.

Here are some simple steps that have helped me:

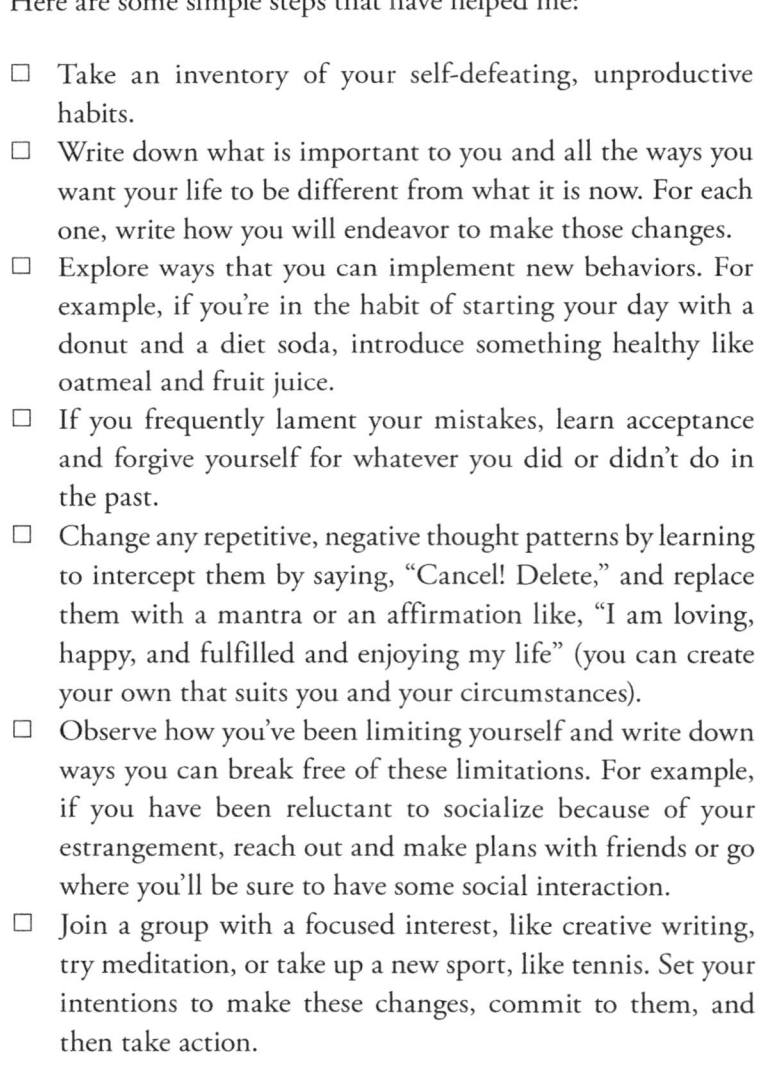

- ☐ Take an inventory of your self-defeating, unproductive habits.
- ☐ Write down what is important to you and all the ways you want your life to be different from what it is now. For each one, write how you will endeavor to make those changes.
- ☐ Explore ways that you can implement new behaviors. For example, if you're in the habit of starting your day with a donut and a diet soda, introduce something healthy like oatmeal and fruit juice.
- ☐ If you frequently lament your mistakes, learn acceptance and forgive yourself for whatever you did or didn't do in the past.
- ☐ Change any repetitive, negative thought patterns by learning to intercept them by saying, "Cancel! Delete," and replace them with a mantra or an affirmation like, "I am loving, happy, and fulfilled and enjoying my life" (you can create your own that suits you and your circumstances).
- ☐ Observe how you've been limiting yourself and write down ways you can break free of these limitations. For example, if you have been reluctant to socialize because of your estrangement, reach out and make plans with friends or go where you'll be sure to have some social interaction.
- ☐ Join a group with a focused interest, like creative writing, try meditation, or take up a new sport, like tennis. Set your intentions to make these changes, commit to them, and then take action.

- ☐ When you find yourself thinking about the story of being abandoned, find a way to gently put it aside. Change your thought, write out some affirmations, and find an activity to distract you, like watering your plants or baking cookies.
- ☐ Ask yourself what makes you happy, what inspires you, and what lifts you up. Use your imagination, be creative, have fun.
- ☐ Strive for peace through such practices as prayer or meditation. Look at the big picture of your life: Do you believe in a divine intelligence, a higher power? Do you believe there is a reason for whatever happens to you? Do you believe that you are a spiritual being temporarily experiencing life in the body?
- ☐ Let go of all negative beliefs you have about yourself. Dig deep; do what is necessary to change your story by replacing hurt and sadness with self-respect and love for yourself and for others.
- ☐ Focus on what you have, not on what you don't have; focus on what you *can* do, not on what you can't do.
- ☐ Be aware of any gifts and blessings you may be taking for granted; acknowledge them and be grateful.

It takes work, but it can be exciting to consider new, exciting possibilities by rewriting your story. Why not make it a happy one? It's up to you.

71. The Beauty around You

The perception of beauty is subjective, as expressed in the saying, "Beauty is in the eye of the beholder." It's also true that through the ages, our notions of beauty change. But what seems to be universal is that we all have a personal experience of beauty, no matter where or when it occurs or whatever the concept.

When caught up in mourning the relationship we once had with our adult child and grandchildren, we often lose the ability to see and appreciate what's right in front of our eyes. However, while we have suffered an enormous loss, there is still much life and beauty all around us.

There are things you may want to start noticing again, like the small buds of flowers unfurling after a long winter, the phases of the moon, and the glimmer of candlelight. Relish the taste of a strawberry, listen to the lush harmonies of a Bach cantata, smell the fresh morning air, or rest your eyes on the new green of spring.

There is beauty everywhere, if you look for it.

Ralph Waldo Emerson said, "Never lose an opportunity of seeing anything that is beautiful; for beauty is God's handwriting—a wayside sacrament. Welcome it in every fair face, in every fair sky, in every fair flower, and thank God for it as a cup of blessing."

Open your eyes, your heart, and your spirit. You will find and experience so much beauty it will amaze you. Drink it in, embrace it, derive joy from it. And don't forget to appreciate that dear, beautiful face you see every day in the mirror.

72. Self-Validation

> Stop looking outside for scraps of pleasure of fulfillment, for validation, security, or love—you have a treasure within that is infinitely greater than anything the world can offer.
>
> —Eckhart Tolle

One of the most important things to develop is self-respect. You are in your own company every day of your life, so you might as well make it good company.

When you were invalidated by your adult child, a part of you may have begun to doubt yourself. Were these accusations from your beloved child true? Were you seeing yourself objectively and in the correct light?

So often in my life, I looked to others to validate me. It took me years to recognize this and many more years to undo my need for approval. I have learned that no one can validate or invalidate me without my permission. My self-respect and happiness are my responsibility.

In the words of writer Somerset Maugham, "Man's desire for the approval of his fellows is so strong, his dread of their censure so violent, that he himself has brought his enemy (conscience) within his gates; and it keeps watch over him, vigilant always in the interests of its master to crush any half-formed desire to break away from the herd." In other words, when you let another's opinion of you direct your beliefs or actions, it's difficult to be true to yourself. You may find that, because of being estranged, you fear rejection more than before. As a result, your behavior may have degenerated into people-pleasing or shying away from social gatherings in order to avoid any interaction.

There are loving, kind, and compassionate people who will help you get back to a sense of yourself. It is okay to ask them for support while you rebuild your strength and good opinion of yourself. While doing this, also practice your positive self-talk. Remind yourself of all the wonderful things you've done in your life and all the ways you've forgiven others and loved them unconditionally.

Honor your efforts. Show compassion for the mistakes you've made, and forgive yourself. Appreciate your inherent goodness and all you have done to elevate yourself and others.

Above all, love yourself; there is no better validation.

> Dare to love yourself as if you were a rainbow with gold at both ends.
> —Aberjhani

73. Comfort in Small Miracles

> I am beginning to learn that it is the sweet, simple things of life which are the real ones after all.
> —Laura Ingalls Wilder

Years ago, when I was going through a difficult time, a friend suggested that I pay attention to and appreciate the small miracles in my life, like relishing each bite of a juicy apple or enjoying the feeling of fresh, clean sheets. This was good advice. I have found it remarkably effective and calming during this estrangement, giving me something else to focus on besides my problems. It is a practice that is beautiful in its simplicity.

When we're in crisis and severely compromised, we often ignore the fundamental blessings inherent in our daily lives. If we can find the strength to look around us, even in the midst of the drama and pain we're experiencing, it's amazing how much there is to appreciate.

Walt Whitman wrote, "Seeing, hearing and feeling are miracles, and each part and tag of me is a miracle." How often do we marvel at the fact that we can feel, see, hear, smell, touch, and taste? That we can bend over and tie our shoelaces, cook a meal, ride a bike, or draw a picture?

It is profoundly helpful to take stock of all we take for granted because it changes our perspective. We become more grateful for all that we have, for all that we've done, seen, and experienced. We become thankful for our health, for food on the table, and for the comforts of home. We take nothing for granted and are thankful for just about everything.

We may not be able to completely eliminate the torment of estrangement, but by shifting our attention, we can ease the pain by appreciating the countless big little miracles that grace our everyday lives.

> There are two ways to live: you can live as if nothing
> is a miracle; you can live as if everything is a miracle.
> —Albert Einstein

74. When to Walk Away

> One day you will ask me which is more important?
> My life or yours? I will say mine and you will walk
> away not knowing that you are my life.
> —Kahlil Gibran

In the beginning of the estrangement from my son and daughter-in-law, I reasoned, argued, emotionally prostrated myself, and swallowed my pride. I jumped through hoops and walked on eggshells. I was accused, abused, played for a fool, and left in the lurch. I felt like I was in a spinning vortex of insanity while my heart broke into a million pieces.

But I kept reaching out. I texted, wrote emails, composed letters of amends, sent cards and gifts for the grandchildren, all the while hoping for a softening on the part of my son and his wife. Unfortunately, that didn't happen, and instead, I was reprimanded and shunned.

I might have suggested family therapy or mediation, but I didn't. I could have contacted an attorney to learn what my visitation rights were as a grandmother (none), but I didn't. I knew intuitively that it would be futile. So instead, I started therapy. And even then, for the longest time, it was too painful to face the fact that my son and daughter-in-law had banished me from their family.

I became aware that feeling so much grief was a serious threat to my physical and emotional health. All of my efforts at negotiation, cooperation, and reconciliation had failed, so there came a moment when I made the decision to reclaim my life.

That's when I really had to face the enormity of my loss. I understood that, after traveling as long and as far as I had in the dynamic of alienation, I could go no further. I agreed with singer Frank Ocean, who said, "Whatever you do, never run back to what broke you."

The most difficult, gut-wrenching decision any parent can make is whether to continue to engage with and accept abuse from a beloved adult child or disconnect from them. When you can no longer function in such an unhealthy relationship, you will come to a crossroads. You'll recognize that it's time to cut the cord between you and your grown child, to walk away from the insanity and begin to do the real work necessary for your transformation and healing. It is the work of honestly admitting that you did all you could to change the situation, but now you must let go. It is the work of turning to yourself and finding sustenance within your own being. It is the work of putting yourself back together, designing and building a new mental and emotional home in which to live that will comfort, sustain, and shelter you, no matter how many storms threaten to blow down your door.

With time and effort, you will find sanctuary within your own heart and soul. And that is the only real refuge there is.

> Sometimes walking away has nothing to do with weakness, and everything to do with strength. We walk away not because we want others to realize our worth and value, but because we finally realize our own.
>
> —Robert Tew

75. Finding Solace

> My soul can find no staircase to Heaven unless it be through Earth's loveliness.
>
> —Michelangelo

The phenomenon of estrangement is coming out in the open. It's a new frontier, with no known effective or proven treatments. There are few support groups that have stood the test of time and just a handful of books on the subject, so it is necessary to discover ways to comfort and heal ourselves.

Along the way, I have learned how to console myself. In the beginning were the basics, like a cup of tea, comfort food, a soft robe, a rocking chair, and hot baths. Later, I found comfort in a spiritual quest that turned into a gradual transformation and awakening of my soul.

Whatever stage you are at in your estrangement, it's important to find relief and consolation, such as burning incense to create a lovely aroma in your home, playing beautiful music, sharing your thoughts and feelings with a close friend, or having a good, cleansing cry. You might start writing in a journal, doing art therapy, or creating a blog. And as I mentioned before, I recommend venturing out into nature and the great outdoors as salve for an aching heart.

Anne Frank, in her young wisdom, wrote, "The best remedy for those who are afraid, lonely, or unhappy is to go outside, somewhere where they can be quiet, alone with the heavens, nature and God.

Because only then does one feel that all is as it should be and that God wishes to see people happy amidst the simple beauty of nature."

One day, I was out walking and came across a meadow of wildflowers. I stopped, transfixed. I tilted my face toward the warmth of the sun. A soft breeze whispered around me as I watched clouds changing shape and butterflies fluttering their gorgeous wings. I was overcome by a sense of wonder, a momentary solace, and to my surprise, I experienced a surge of joy.

It was then I knew that I had begun to heal.

> It is astounding how little the ordinary person notices butterflies.
> —Vladimir Nabokov

76. Building Character and Strength

> Moral excellence comes about as a result of habit. We become just by doing just acts, temperate by doing temperate acts, brave by doing brave acts.
> —Aristotle

We admire people who are courageous and honest. You may think, yes, I want that, I want to be like that person ... but how? I'm doing my best, and I still seem to fall short.

Like everything else, building character and strength takes awareness and commitment to practice. We have been brought down by the events in our lives, and we need time to process them. But we tend to be impatient with ourselves. For example, we wonder why we continue to feel so despondent over the loss of our families after a good amount of time has passed. Well, it's understandable that we would feel despondent; we've lost a relationship with one or more of our loved ones.

Being strong and resilient means understanding that sometimes we don't feel very strong and resilient. We all fall down, get scared, and run for cover at times. When that happens, we must strive to be patient and compassionate with ourselves. There are many pitfalls in the dynamics of estrangement, and the work that needs to be done, if we choose to do the work, is daunting.

Leonardo da Vinci said, "The depth and strength of a human character are defined by its moral reserves. People reveal themselves completely only when they are thrown out of the customary conditions of their life, for only then do they have to fall back on their reserves."

There were times when I felt so beaten up, I was inconsolable. But, finally, I decided that when I felt the need to cry, I'd let myself, but as soon as I tossed the last tissue into the trash, I'd get busy with an activity. For example, going to the gym or riding my bike to the farmers market for fresh produce worked wonders and gave me a feeling of being in control of my environment and mood.

Be honest with yourself. Reflect on your behaviors, your desires, and your habits. Admit to any defects of character, without judgement, and change them. Dig deep and get clear on what drives and motivates you.

With every new insight, discovery, and healthy change you make, you grow stronger and happier to be in your own shoes. You begin to have a love affair with yourself because you are building character and strength, which is a gift to yourself and to all who know you.

You become the person you want to be.

> Watch your thoughts, for they become words.
> Watch your words, for they become actions.
> Watch your actions, for they become habits.
> Watch your habits, for they become character.
> Watch your character, for it becomes your destiny.
> —Author Unknown

77. Collateral Damage

> People at war with themselves will always cause collateral damage in the lives of those around them.
> —John Mark Green

Being alienated by our adult child is difficult, but even more disturbing is the fact that there are innocent victims: our grandchildren.

How are the children handling our absence? What are they being told about us?

Children have the right to know their grandparents. Unfortunately, in the case of alienation, they are victims of their parents' incomprehensible decision to deprive them of a normal, loving relationship with their grandparents. This is unfair and damaging to the children and results in confusion and loss for them. Most importantly, they are missing out on an important archetypal relationship with grandparents who love them dearly.

Alex Haley wrote, "Nobody can do for little children what grandparents do. Grandparents sort of sprinkle stardust over the lives of little children." It's true: Grandparents typically shower their grandchildren with an unconditional love that is unique to them. They are usually free to love wholeheartedly with available time, attention, and patience. It's a beautiful gift to the grandchildren but, in the case of alienation, one that has been heartlessly stolen from them.

Everyone is affected, and everyone suffers. No grandparent

deserves such cruelty, and no grandchild deserves to be cut off from loving grandparents. In the words of Margaret Mead, "Everyone needs to have access both to both grandparents and grandchildren in order to be a full human being."

Since we can't change the situation, the following may help mitigate the unfortunate effects of the estrangement:

- ☐ Keep a journal in which you write about how much you love and miss your grandchildren.
- ☐ Keep photos of yourself and your ancestors in an album or scrapbook for them.
- ☐ Write about who you are and about your family.
- ☐ Send gifts for birthdays and holidays if they are allowed to accept them.
- ☐ Write to them, either by texts, emails, or letters.
- ☐ Make videos of yourself talking to the grandchildren, sharing your thoughts and feelings, and save them for a later date.
- ☐ Send your love to your grandchildren energetically, from your heart to theirs. Imagine them happy, healthy, and basking in the warmth of the love that only you can give them.
- ☐ Get on with your life, with hope and love in your heart.

After so many years, I still feel the agony of being wrenched from my grandchildren's lives. I only hope there will come a time when they understand that since our separation began—that terrible day when even the angels cried—I have never stopped loving them.

> There is a big difference between being a proper parent who protects a child from danger and being a dictator who psychologically abuses their child through lies and deceit in order to control every detail of their life and alienate loving grandparents.
> —Carolyn Smith

78. Transcending Pain

> Find a place inside where there's joy, and the joy will burn out the pain.
>
> —Joseph Campbell

As we get older, many of us live with chronic physical pain. We may have arthritis, old injuries that flare up, or issues with backache or sciatica. We learn to accept the discomfort and can often manage it through exercise, body work, a healthy diet, stress-reduction techniques, and good sleep. The pain may never completely go away, but ultimately, we can learn to live with it and not let it defeat us.

Estrangement causes emotional pain that is debilitating and chronic. At first, we're not equipped to handle it, and unlike a physical problem, there is no real remedy or therapy for this kind of emotional agony. We are left to our own devices, with no idea what to do, where to go, or how to get there.

Those of us with both physical and emotional pain have a twofold challenge: Physical problems can exacerbate emotional pain, and emotional pain can cause or intensify physical problems.

A while ago, I had an accident that broke my back. There have been several repercussions, like the onset of migraines, which have compounded my depression. The perfect storm of physical, emotional, and mental distress can make for a pretty miserable state of mind. As Will Rogers observed, "Pain is such an uncomfortable feeling that even a tiny amount of it is enough to ruin every enjoyment."

What to do?

In my experience, it's all about managing the variety and levels of pain. If you're experiencing physical pain, you can find doctors or holistic practitioners to help ameliorate your symptoms and ease your discomfort. Managing psychic, emotional pain, however, is a bit trickier.

As much as I work on healing from estrangement and alienation, I am always aware of an underlying emotional pain, like a constant buzzing in the background. Whatever happens in my life is colored by grief that crouches in the shadows and never seems to leave me.

Having said that, I have discovered ways to cope, move forward, and experience joy again. Here are some ideas that might help you:

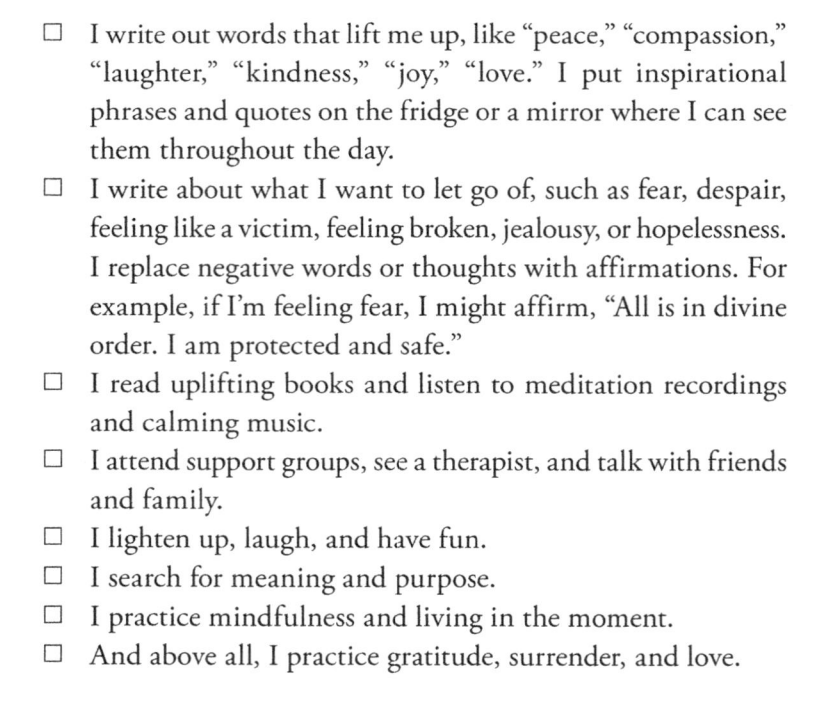

- ☐ I write out words that lift me up, like "peace," "compassion," "laughter," "kindness," "joy," "love." I put inspirational phrases and quotes on the fridge or a mirror where I can see them throughout the day.
- ☐ I write about what I want to let go of, such as fear, despair, feeling like a victim, feeling broken, jealousy, or hopelessness. I replace negative words or thoughts with affirmations. For example, if I'm feeling fear, I might affirm, "All is in divine order. I am protected and safe."
- ☐ I read uplifting books and listen to meditation recordings and calming music.
- ☐ I attend support groups, see a therapist, and talk with friends and family.
- ☐ I lighten up, laugh, and have fun.
- ☐ I search for meaning and purpose.
- ☐ I practice mindfulness and living in the moment.
- ☐ And above all, I practice gratitude, surrender, and love.

It's not easy to experience both physical and emotional pain. It's not easy to find ways to cope, find comfort, and live a joyful life. But it *is* easy to stay stuck in a rut where the longer you stay, the tougher it is to climb out. Eckhart Tolle writes, "Pain can only feed on pain. Pain cannot feed on joy. It finds it quite indigestible."

Finding ways to manage your physical and emotional pain will help you live your best life and find joy again.

> We either make ourselves miserable or we make ourselves strong. The amount of work is the same.
> —Carlos Castenada

79. Creating a Vision for Your Life

> Pursue some path, however narrow and crooked, in which you can walk with love and reverence.
> —Henry David Thoreau

This time without your grandchildren can potentially open up areas of your life you never would have explored otherwise. Chances are you have more time and energy to spare now, and finding new outlets for your talents and interests can be therapeutic.

Carl Jung observed, "Your vision will become clear only when you can look into your own heart. Who looks outside, dreams; who looks inside, awakes." What gets your juices flowing? What are your gifts? What is meaningful, exciting, fulfilling, creative, and fun to you? Is there anything that you've always wanted to do that you never found the time or energy to explore?

Too often, we prevent ourselves from accomplishing what we'd like because we are unmotivated or afraid of failure. Maybe you've secretly wanted to write a book, do stand-up comedy, or learn to make balloon animals. Whatever it is, what are you waiting for?

Estrangement changes not only your day-to-day life but also your worldview. To avoid becoming embittered and negative, explore your interests, passions, and talents. Write them down and prioritize the various activities that appeal to you. Read your list on a daily basis, hone it, and visualize yourself doing these things. Do some research, investigate opportunities, and then take action. Becoming proactive makes it easier to maintain a positive attitude and perspective, while having the additional benefit of getting your mind off your troubles.

British writer James Allen described it this way: "The greatest achievement was at first and for a time a dream. The oak sleeps in the acorn, the bird waits in the egg, and in the highest vision of the soul a waking angel stirs. Dreams are the seedlings of realities."

I spent a lot of time feeling defeated and depressed after being separated from my grandchildren. If anyone had suggested that I find things to do that I felt passionate about, I would have dismissed them out of hand. I barely had enough energy to wash my hair, let alone sign up for an exciting new class.

Then, one evening, I was sitting around, watching some mindless TV show, when I realized I was wasting my life. I got up, turned off the TV, and said out loud, "Enough!" I went online and signed up for a music ensemble class at the local college. Then I contacted a fellow pianist, and now we get together and play duets at least once a week. I'm having fun; remember fun? And I am committed to enjoying my life, even if I must do so without my family.

Create a new vision for your life, and get busy making your dreams come true. To paraphrase from William Earnest Henley's poem, *Invictus*, you are the master of your fate; you are the captain of your soul. Decide what is important to you, use your imagination, and express yourself. For instance, if you feel like wearing a sombrero and big clown shoes to the supermarket, do it. Jump out of your comfort zone, and get excited about your life.

In the words of Auntie Mame (by Patrick Dennis), "Life is a banquet, and most poor suckers are starving to death." There is so much more to life than just existing. It can be rich and amazing, but only *you* can create the life you want.

80. Your Home, Your Sanctuary

> Where is home? Home is where the heart can laugh without shyness. Home is where the heart's tears can dry at their own pace.
>
> —Vernon Baker

When you come home after a long day, do you feel a sense of peace when you walk through your door? Do you let out a sigh of contentment as you put your keys away and look around you? Is your home visually pleasing, with inviting chairs, soft fabrics, and fluffy pillows? Is your kitchen warm and welcoming? Have you surrounded yourself with things you love, like candles, books, and pictures? How does your home smell, sound, and feel? Is it a refuge, a place where you can recharge and enjoy some much-needed tranquility?

"If we could make our house a home, and then make it a sanctuary, I think we could truly find paradise on Earth," observed lifestyle author Alexandra Stoddard. Now that I must live my days without my son and grandchildren, my home environment is more important to me than ever. Along with other chosen objects I enjoy, I always derive comfort from nature inside and out, from the sight of trees outside my window to the white orchid gracing my living room. I keep only what pleases me. If there is a book, picture, or piece of clothing that I am ambivalent about, I either put it away or give it away. If there is something that evokes a painful memory, I get rid of it. Only that which brings comfort and beauty is welcome in my home.

When I recently did a spring cleaning in my house, I decided that it was time to go through old pictures and boxes filled with mementos. I had been putting this chore off for years, because I knew it would be heartrending to travel down memory lane. As I sifted through old photos of my son and me and my grandchildren as babies, I felt very sad. I came across pictures my grandkids had drawn for me, along with sweet cards and letters. I took my time looking at everything and allowed myself to feel the feelings that came up, and I had a good, cleansing cry.

I had held onto the boxes of memories long enough. I didn't need to see pictures, drawings, cards, and letters from the past because they only caused me sorrow. So I carefully wrapped up photos from my son's childhood and sent them to him. I threw away many drawings, cards, and anything else that were reminders of all that I had lost.

Look around you. Are there any photos on display that bring up sadness in you? Are there any boxes that need sorting? Could your kitchen counter use a bowl of fresh fruit? Some cut flowers on a table? How about your bedroom? Do you love your bed, your linens, the colors? Do you have plush towels and fragrant soaps in your bathroom? Do you have comfortable furniture in your living spaces, a functional desk, good lighting?

The interior of your home is an inside garden, and like an outside garden, it requires frequent tending and loving attention. It can be a fulfilling practice and also great fun.

There is no better time than now to create your sanctuary. You need solace, serenity, and daily physical reminders that life can be peaceful, beautiful, and enriching.

Make your home your refuge.

> He is the happiest, be he king or peasant, who finds peace in his home.
> —Johann Wolfgang von Goethe

81. Slaying the Dragons within You

> Heroes take journeys, confront dragons, and discover the treasure of their true selves.
> —Carol Pearson

We often turn to others for love and support because we don't trust or love ourselves enough. But by looking to someone else, we may be asking for the impossible because, like us, they also may be looking for love and support and therefore cannot give us what they don't have to give. Ultimately, it all comes down to loving ourselves.

Many of us learned as children to rely on others for our safety and well-being. As a result, many of us never learned how to comfort ourselves and find the love inside that would sustain us throughout our lives.

If we don't know how to take care of ourselves—physically, emotionally, and spiritually—we will always be looking for someone else to fill our empty places. For example, if we make our happiness dependent on our adult child's behavior, they will inadvertently control us. If they don't call, we're sad; if they do call, we're delighted. It's a dysfunctional merry-go-round, and it doesn't stop until we decide to jump off, plant our feet firmly on the ground, and make some serious changes within ourselves.

Only *you* can heroically slay the dragons of fear, anger, jealousy, resentment, hurt, and sadness that devour your vitality. It's a strenuous undertaking to overcome years of conditioning and false beliefs about your worthiness and goodness. Start slowly, by observing your thoughts, feelings, and beliefs. For instance, when you catch yourself feeling envious or resentful, set about redirecting your thoughts. Be in control of your mind and emotions by utilizing positive self-talk. The more you do this, the stronger you will become. Know that you can change.

This work requires forgiveness: of yourself and of others. It involves looking deeply and honestly at who you really are and not only facing the truth of that but embracing it. It requires letting go, starting fresh, and appreciating every precious, fleeting moment.

There is a wonderful quote by writer Brian Andreas: "Anyone can slay a dragon … but try waking up every morning and loving the world all over again. That's what takes a real hero."

Every day, refuse to give power to the dragons within you, and fight the good fight to eradicate neediness, fear, and lack of self-respect. Call up the love you have for yourself, for others, and for your life. Enjoy a new independence, where you want nothing more than to give from your true and loving heart.

> We're our own dragons as well as our own heroes,
> and we have to rescue ourselves from ourselves.
> —Tom Robbins

82. As Time Goes By

> It's only when we truly know and understand that we have a limited time on earth—and that we have no way of knowing when our time is up—that we will begin to live each day to the fullest, as if it was the only one we had.
> —Elisabeth Kübler-Ross

Recently, I was greeted by a receptionist who, after exchanging hellos, sighed and said, "At least we're halfway there." When I looked puzzled, she said, "It's Wednesday. Only two more days until Friday."

I remember feeling that way when I was younger and working six days a week. It seemed that the work week would never end. Now, weeks seem to fly by, and I have a sense of poignancy when each day draws to a close.

Even though you may be facing many challenges and heartbreaks, each new day is still an extraordinary gift. It's a miracle to have lived this long and to have experienced the laughter, the joy, and, yes, the heartaches and the tears.

What if we believed that we are here on earth for a reason and that we are more than our bodies, our kids, our houses, our cars, our money? It's so easy to get caught up in the everyday activities, worries, joys, and heartbreaks of life. We often lose sight of a larger perspective, one that has its precepts rooted in acceptance, letting go, forgiveness, gratitude, and love. By embracing these concepts, our lives undergo a metamorphosis. We are more able to meet our challenges and can accept the agonies and the ecstasies. And finally, one day, we realize that a deeper wisdom has dawned within us.

I love this quote from Rumi:

> Today, like every other day, we wake up empty and frightened.
> Don't open the door to the study and begin reading.
> Take down a musical instrument.

It is possible to choose happiness over suffering. By making a paradigm shift from the belief that everything is difficult and that life is mostly suffering to a belief that life is an amazing adventure that is over too soon, we will be healthier, feel happier, and have a lot more fun.

After enough time has been spent living in sadness and grief, we can decide to turn away from it and make the best of a bad situation. We can choose to manage our expectations, surrender to and accept what we can't change, and treasure our time on this earth.

> Of time you would make a stream upon whose
> bank you would sit and watch its flowing.
> Yet the timeless in you is aware of life's timelessness,
> And knows that yesterday is but today's memory
> and tomorrow is today's dream.
> And that which sings and contemplates in you
> is still dwelling within the bounds of that first
> moment which scattered the stars into space.
> —Kahlil Gibran

83. And Still You Rise

Many people feel more compassion for others than they do for themselves. We have empathy for people who are challenged in life, and we extend understanding for their failings and shortcomings. But we often don't extend that same consideration to ourselves.

You did the best you could at the time, and if you'd known better, you would have done better. This statement has great validity and is a good one to remember whenever you feel regret, sadness, or guilt about the past.

You have been disrespected by your adult child or whoever is responsible for alienating and estranging you. You've blamed yourself, doubted yourself, abandoned yourself, maligned yourself, and hurt yourself. Despite this, you've kept on going. How many times during these weeks, months, or years of estrangement have you wanted to pack it in and give up? There may have been days you didn't want to leave your house because you were too depressed or exhausted, but you kept on, putting one foot in front of the other. And every time you got out of bed, splashed your face with cold water, walked out your front door, and continued on with your life, you developed stronger mental and emotional muscles.

Spiritual teacher Gary Zukav writes, "We cannot stop the winter or the summer from coming. We cannot stop the spring or the fall or make them other than they are. They are gifts from the universe that we cannot refuse. But we can choose what we will contribute to life when each arrives."

There were days when I didn't want to get out of bed. It just didn't seem worth the trouble. I had so many heartaches, they had to form a line. One morning as I lay in bed ruminating and bemoaning everything that had gone wrong in my life, I swiftly and deliberately put the brakes on the negativity. I chose five things I felt profoundly grateful for: the ease of my breath, my beautiful home near the sea, the breeze coming through the window, my good health, and my still beating heart. As I took several deep breaths, I reminded myself that I was doing my best to transform my life, one day at a time, and that was enough. Then I got up, opened the shades, and thanked the gods for a beautiful day.

"Do what you can, with what you have, where you are," said Theodore Roosevelt. Let go of perfectionism, self-blame, and self-criticism. Instead, tell yourself that you did your best, if you'd known better you would have done better, and you're doing your best *now*.

With each day, you are healing your brokenness. Yes, there are times when you feel you can't continue, but you can because you're becoming stronger and wiser. Let go of constant sorrow, and fill the cracks in your heart with the healing gold of compassion, forgiveness, and love.

> You may shoot me with your words,
> You may cut me with your eyes,
> You may kill me with your hatefulness,
> But still, like air, I'll rise.
> —Maya Angelou, *Still I Rise*

84. Blessing Others

> Bless them that curse you.
> Matthew 5:44

It has been a rough road. You have felt every conceivable emotion and done everything you could to build a bridge between you and your alienators. But since you were unable to expedite healing and reconciliation, you've had to learn acceptance in order to move forward in your life.

Now that you've come to this point of understanding and forbearance, there is one more thing you might consider doing: Bless those who have hurt you.

What does it mean to bless someone? It means that you deliberately and sincerely wish the best for them. It is a spiritually based practice, not a religious one. You free yourself from negative thoughts or feelings about someone and focus on their goodness and the fact that they are doing the best they can in this life.

You may wonder how you can possibly do this; you can. If you're thinking this is ridiculous and delusional, it's not. Yes, you have been hurt, but why carry the weight of this any longer?

Mother Teresa said, "Some people come in your life as blessings. Some come in your life as lessons." If you curse those who have hurt you and walk around with anger and resentment eating you up, you only poison yourself. By doing this, you increase the probability for emotional outbursts, depression, and other health problems. You can choose to hold on to your misery, but what good will it do? You'll just waste your life. Instead, bless your alienators. By blessing them, you release them. It may seem counterintuitive, but by doing this, you increase your own happiness. Author Mary Anne Radmacher said, "As we work to create light for others, we naturally light our own way."

I remember when I first had the thought of sending blessings to my son and daughter-in-law, my second thought was, *Why would I do that? Look what they've put me through.* It soon became clear to me that blessing them was exactly what I needed to do to release myself from the resentment I felt. It took time, and I still struggle with letting go of anger and hurt, but when I can get out of my own way, it's a relief to simply bless them, forgive them, and let them go.

85. Gratitude

> He is a wise man who does not grieve for the things which he has not, but rejoices for those which he has.
> —Epictetus

One morning, I took my dog for a hike up a hill overlooking a canyon ablaze with daisies and black-eyed Susans. I sat for a while, simply enjoying the sun, the cool breeze, and the scenery. Out of nowhere, a hawk flew into the canyon, gliding on the wind currents. It was suspended for several minutes, almost completely still. Then, it suddenly swooped up and down, like it was dancing on the wind. It was a wonderful sight, and I felt grateful to have witnessed such beauty.

In the words of the poet Rumi, "Be grateful for whatever comes because each has been sent as a guide from beyond." Think of the gifts, the blessings, and the graces you have in your life: a working mind, a healthy body, talents, a vibrant spirit, hard lessons, easy lessons, work, play, laughter, tears, children running barefoot on summer grass, music, art, stories around campfires, bicycles, movies, swimming pools, playgrounds, ice cream cones, loving hands caressing your face, clouds, rain, mountains, sequoias, wildflowers, hummingbirds, and the wonder of a sunrise and a sunset, beginning and ending each day on this amazing earth.

"Reflect upon your present blessings, of which every man has plenty; not on your past misfortunes, of which all men have some," wrote Charles Dickens. To that end, and despite the ongoing reality of being separated from my grandchildren, I am happier now than I have been in years. It's not the happiness I experienced before being alienated from my grandchildren, but it's a happiness that has evolved from integrating acceptance, humility, surrender, and gratitude. I am optimizing my sense of wellness and peace of mind by making it a daily practice to emphasize my blessings, which helps to de-emphasizes the sorrows. Oh, the sadness still lurks in the shadows, waiting to pounce. But by focusing on gratitude, I keep the blues at bay and go on with as much faith, optimism, and appreciation as I can muster.

There are many ongoing challenges and heartaches relating to estrangement, but it is nevertheless possible, through everyday gratitude, to find happiness, even during this time of disconnection from our loved ones. "The struggle ends when the gratitude begins," writes Neale Donald Walsch. This is true.

Life is amazingly, astonishingly precious, and by practicing gratitude for all it has given us, it becomes even more so.

> I thank You God for most this amazing
> day: for the leaping greenly spirits of trees
> and a blue true dream of sky; and for everything
> which is natural which is infinite which is yes.
> —e.e. cummings

86. No Stone Left Unturned

Leaving no stone unturned is, of course, an idiom for doing everything possible to find a solution to a problem in order to bring about the best outcome.

As a parent and grandparent who has experienced abandonment and estrangement, you have undoubtedly done everything within your power to restore order and stability in your family dynamic. You reached out but were silenced, and you tacitly accepted the unacceptable. You reasoned, amended, listened, refuted. You were tried and found guilty of crimes not committed and were ultimately sentenced to a life ostracized from your loved ones. You desperately searched for a way back to your former status of being an integral part of your family, but unfortunately, your efforts to communicate failed to appease your alienators. You became entangled in a rigged game where the odds were stacked against you. Finally, it became masochistic to continue pursuing a relationship with those who undermined you, disrespected you, and repeatedly pushed you away.

Epictetus wrote, "First say to yourself what you would be; and then do what you have to do." Unless you want to remain disempowered and disenfranchised, you must get up and start again. You must turn your back on the lies, abuse, and insanity and find something to live for besides your adult child and grandchildren. You must choose between continuing to live a life of being marginalized and beginning a new life of dignity and self-respect. In the words of psychoanalyst Anna Freud, "I was always looking outside myself for strength and confidence, but it comes from within. It is there all of the time."

Not every obstacle can be removed, and not every battle can be won. Sometimes, we fail. If you feel you have done all you can to expedite reconciliation, that you have left no stone unturned and you can do no more, then accept things as they are. You did everything possible to bring love to a loveless and unfortunate state of affairs. Let this be your great opportunity, your teachable moment, to let go and to find peace.

> Not being able to govern events, I govern myself.
> —Michel de Montaigne

87. Being the Hero of Your Story

> Life has no smooth road for any of us; and in the bracing atmosphere of a high aim the very roughness stimulates the climber to steadier steps, till the legend, over steep ways to the stars, fulfills itself.
> —W. C. Doane

We are always being challenged to grow. It can be uncomfortable but is necessary if we want to learn acceptance, find peace, and attain wisdom.

Typical by-products of alienation and estrangement are bruised feelings and wounded hearts. We spend days, months, even years in confusion, hurt, and despair, with no idea where to turn. Although grieving is a necessary part of the healing process, there comes a pivotal point when we must reset our internal GPS. We either choose to remain stuck in the inertia of grief or move away from it and start down a new path, one that is waiting for our fresh footprints.

I became fed up with the emotional rut I was in, due to habitual negative thinking, and began to reshape my thoughts. I deliberately changed unproductive attitudes and beliefs to new ideas about what I've done in my life and who I am. I switched from guilt and shame to compassion and enthusiasm. At times, it felt like an impossible task to turn this ship around toward a different horizon, because I'd been stuck in fear, hurt, and negativity for so long.

I started by changing not only my internal self-talk but also my external talk: I stopped talking with friends about being banished from my son's family. I stopped beating that dead horse and, instead, chose subjects of mutual interest, like books, movies, the arts, current events, health, and spirituality. I made new friends. I explored new ideas, found new places to visit, and signed up for volunteer work. My worldview expanded and became more positive.

By making changes, we explore our depths and heights, and we discover our own truths. We unearth mental and emotional strengths we never knew existed within us. We have more satisfying relationships and experiences.

We can't always control what happens in our lives, but we can choose our responses. If we fall into a dark and scary emotional pit, we can either be paralyzed by fear or we can choose to heroically fight the monsters and climb out of the hole, Indiana Jones-style.

"Opportunities to find deeper powers within ourselves come when life seems most challenging," explained mythologist Joseph Campbell, who wrote about the hero's journey in *The Power of Myth* and other books. By choosing a hero's journey, we face the adventures of life head on, eyes wide open, and cold sober. This takes courage. As we meet the challenges inherent in any worthwhile endeavor, we learn tenacity, discernment, and optimism, and we discover that there is strength in humility.

When we finally emerge from the morass of grief and soak in the warm rays of self-love, peace, and acceptance, we are forever changed. Wiser, stronger, and more in harmony with our own nature, we become the hero of our story.

> Above all, be the heroine of your life, not the victim.
> —Nora Ephron

88. Keeping It Real

> The Dude abides.
> —*The Big Lebowski*

I have more good days now. But, surprisingly, even though the bad days are less frequent, they are still pretty intense. Maybe it's because the estrangement from my family has been going on for so long. Maybe it's because my grandchildren have entered adolescence, and it's official: I've missed their childhoods. Maybe it's the moral indignation I feel as a result of the staggering cruelty of being forced to give up a normal relationship with my grandkids. There is so much I wish I could share with them. Author and poet May Sarton wrote, "There is only one real deprivation … and that is not to be able to give one's gifts to those one loves most."

Due to the miracles of technology, I am occasionally in touch with the two oldest grandchildren through texting. I am glad about it but admit to a certain aching ambivalence. While I am grateful for this virtual contact with the kids, I don't know them, and because of this, I feel bereft and depressed after communicating with them. It just seems surreal that I'm permitted to communicate via texts but not allowed to see them in person.

Although it's true that I am slowly changing my thinking, taking it one day at a time and endeavoring to create peace in my life, the wounds haven't healed. Not a single a day goes by when I don't mourn the loss of the relationship I once had with my son or feel the absence of my grandchildren. But every day, I get closer to accepting the reality that the dream of being a part of my grandchildren's childhoods is over.

It's time to get real, to go deeper into surrender and acceptance. It's time to stop thinking about them and release myself from this angst. It's time I created a new dream, one that doesn't include my son and grandchildren. Someday, if they come back into my life, I will welcome them with open arms. Until then, like the Dude, I will simply abide.

> Respect your efforts, respect yourself. Self-respect leads to self-discipline. When you have both firmly under your belt, that's real power.
> —Clint Eastwood

89. Forgiveness

> Forgiveness is the fragrance that the violet sheds on the heel that has crushed it.
> —Mark Twain

It's not always easy to forgive others, but to do so is to release yourself from the torture of resentment and anger.

That you might resist forgiving your alienators is understandable. After all, their behaviors have been irrational and self-serving, and they have hurt you deeply by callously cutting you out of your grandchildren's lives. But if you stay anchored in outrage and indignation, you will ruin your own life. Inspirational author Catherine Ponder says it well: "When you hold resentment toward another, you are bound to that person or condition by an emotional link that is stronger than steel. Forgiveness is the only way to dissolve that link and get free."

What if you could put yourself in the mind-set of a detached, wise elder and grant clemency to those who are responsible for alienating you from your grandkids? What if you could find a place in your heart to absolve them of all offenses, recognizing that they have their own perspectives, mind-sets, and problems? It's not that you condone or approve of their behavior; it's that you're done with it, done with thinking about it all the time, done with feeling impotent and infuriated, done with holding on to a scorched remnant of the relationship you once had with your child. You're sick of the pain, and you want—no, you *need*—a reprieve.

Lewis B. Smedes, theologian and author, wrote, "To forgive is to set a prisoner free and discover that the prisoner was you." Holding on to blame and resentment sets off a stress response and compromises the health of your body, mind, and spirit. So for your own good, forgive them with an open heart. Stretch yourself and reach for a higher perspective, even a spiritual one. Let go of the past. Let go of bitterness and anger. By holding on, you only hurt yourself. In the words of author Jack Kornfield, "To let go is to release the images and emotions, the grudges and fears, the clingings and disappointments of the past that bind our spirit."

Enter into a loving relationship with yourself, your heart, your higher self. Release those you wish to forgive, and keep on loving them. Remember: This is for *your* freedom and peace of mind.

> I am bigger than the image you have of me.
> I am stronger,
> I am more beautiful,
> And I am infinitely more precious than you thought me.
> I will forgive you.
> My forgiveness is not a gift that I am giving to you.
> When I forgive you
> My forgiveness will be a gift that gives itself to me.
> —Desmond Tutu

90. Practice, Practice, Practice

We always have choices. We can choose happiness or misery. We can choose to numb ourselves with substances and distractions, like alcohol, drugs, junk food, or watching too much TV. Or we can choose to get rid of destructive habits and form new life-affirming ones.

Whatever you choose requires attention and practice. If you want to indulge your sorrows and hurts, especially as it pertains to estrangement from your adult child and grandchildren, your mind will form loops that repeatedly return to thoughts of sadness. The more this happens, the more engrained your thought patterns become, and before you know it, you've formed a habit, a very harmful one. Negative thoughts are powerful and take a toll on your state of mind, your emotions, and your health. Think of it as introducing poison into your system that makes you both physically ill and heartsick.

Bringing about positive change takes time and diligence. Damaging, self-defeating habits are tenacious and tough to expunge. So when you're ready for a revision in your life, start slowly. Notice how often random negative thoughts pop into your head. Pay attention to how often you are taken out of the present by thinking about the past or the future. As you recognize these thoughts, shoo them out and replace them with supportive and comforting ones. Author Dennis Merritt Jones writes, "As a mindfulness practice, become the conscious observer of your thoughts, feelings and actions today. Notice how much of your energy is being stolen from you by the time-bandits of the past and the future."

Here are some important techniques to help achieve positive change in your thoughts and emotions:

- ☐ Beware of all-or-nothing/black-or-white thinking. There is often a middle ground, one where you might gain insights and have compassion for yourself and for your estranged adult child.
- ☐ Catch yourself when you think about the past (which makes you sad) or the future (which creates anxiety). Bring your mind back to the present. You can't change what has already happened, and you cannot predict what will happen.
- ☐ Practice mindfulness by noticing when you step out of reality by catastrophizing events or making up stories about the hows, whys, wheres, or whens.
- ☐ Be consistent and introduce healthy thoughts and behaviors on a daily basis.
- ☐ Practice gratitude. Make gratitude lists, take gratitude walks, and every morning and evening, think of five things you are grateful for.
- ☐ Affirm your life, health, talents, accomplishments, wisdom, goodness, and worth. Have some phrases and affirmations ready when you need them, such as "I am a loving person," "I am living a wonderful, creative, and meaningful life," or "I am vibrantly healthy and am always safe and loved." And believe them.
- ☐ Limit your time talking and thinking about estrangement and find new interests and hobbies.
- ☐ Find meaning and purpose that doesn't revolve around your estranged family members.
- ☐ Have hope for reconciliation while going on with and creating happiness in your own life.
- ☐ Love and accept yourself.

- ☐ Imagine yourself happy without your kids and grandkids. Yes, that's right: *without* them.

In the wise words of Aristotle, "Excellence is an art won by training and habituation. We do not act rightly because we have virtue or excellence, but we rather have those because we have acted rightly. We are what we repeatedly do. Excellence, then, is not an act, but a habit."

I know you miss your grandchildren, but don't waste another minute of your life lamenting what you can't have. Practice hope; practice faith, gratitude, and acceptance. You don't have unlimited time left on this earth, so I urge you to create a fantastic, wonderful life for yourself.

Practice is everything.

> Practice means to perform, over and over again in the face of all obstacles, some act of vision, of faith, of desire. Practice is a means of inviting the perfection desired.
> —Martha Graham

91. Honoring Yourself

> Plant your own garden and decorate your own soul,
> instead of waiting for someone to bring you flowers.
> —Veronica A. Shoffstall

You have suffered a great loss. You are working on healing and doing all you can to rise above the pain. You are processing the tormenting emotions resulting from alienation and estrangement and searching for equilibrium, slowly evolving to a new status quo. You are coming to terms with the fact that you need to create a new normal or risk losing your health and vitality.

You may have been dishonored by your adult child or a son- or daughter-in-law. You may have been lied to or lied about. You may have been disrespected and hurt deeply by their accusations, thoughtlessness, and cruelty. But the bottom line is that your self-respect does not rest on their opinions of you, but on your own personal conviction of your worthiness and value. In the words of Mahatma Gandhi, "They cannot take away our self-respect if we do not give it to them."

There are days when your pain still burns in a fire of loneliness, anguish, and grief, but one day, it will cool to ashes, from which a sacred wisdom and peace will rise up within you. You will honor yourself and all that you have lived through.

Love, honor, and celebrate yourself.

> Loving yourself ... does not mean being self-absorbed or narcissistic, or disregarding others. Rather it means welcoming yourself as the most honored guest in your own heart, a guest worthy of respect, a lovable companion.
>
> —Margot Anand

92. Keeping Hope Alive

One day, you might receive a surprise phone call from your estranged child or an email from your grandchild. In a moment, your life could change.

It may feel like the estrangement you are experiencing will go on forever, but there's a good probability it won't. Everything changes, people have epiphanies, and wrongs are righted. It happens all the time.

What if you knew that in a week, a month, or a year from now, you'd be visiting your grandchildren and actively healing your relationship with your adult child? Are you ready? Have you worked through any emotional encumbrances, like anger, resentment, shame, blame, guilt, and hurt? How about self-defeating behaviors like addictions, people-pleasing, or codependency? For the question is not "How can I change them?" but "How can I change myself?"

Work on building emotional resilience so that you can extend compassion and forgiveness to your adult child. They may or may not take full or even partial responsibility for alienating you from your grandchildren, but if you've worked on yourself, you'll be better able to negotiate from a place of wisdom and love.

Too often, people stay stuck in inertia and despair. Instead of practicing patience and letting events unfold organically, they give up hope too soon. I often hear stories from people who were estranged for many years, when suddenly their adult children and grandchildren came back into their lives. Some families were able to settle their differences quickly; others took more time. Parents who never gave up hope, who worked on improving their own state of mind, and who let go of grievances in the interest of moving forward were the most successful.

In the words of Thich Nhat Hanh, "Hope is important because it can make the present moment less difficult to bear. If we believe that tomorrow will be better, we can bear a hardship today." Our choices are clear: We can hold on to grudges, or we can harbor no ill feelings and be hopeful for a future healing and reconciliation with our child. In the end, after doing everything within our power to restore loving relations, if it doesn't turn out as we hoped, we will at least have a clear conscience. We will be able to accept the outcome and ask no more than what the reality of the situation can offer.

After spending years feeling hopeless and unsure about what to do to improve the situation with my estranged son and his family, I finally had to let go. I turned within, searching for my purpose in life. I had a strong desire to bring the terrible reality of family estrangement out into the open. I started a blog on the subject, which helped me express my thoughts and feelings. When people started writing to me, telling me how much the blog had helped them, it became clear that there are many parents and grandparents in the throes of this kind of tragedy. We are not alone, and there is no need to suffer alone.

Family alienation and estrangement is not only a personal problem but a societal one. By keeping hope alive and helping others keep hope alive, we join together in searching for healthy, loving solutions for us all.

> When you feel like the world's at its end,
> Or when your heart seems to break, unable to mend,
> Never give up hope,
> Because life holds its own beautiful plan.
> —Max Soon

93. Carrying On

> New beginnings are often disguised as painful endings.
>
> —Lao Tzu

You've done your homework. You've cried a million tears, worked on your anger, forgiven yourself, and forgiven others. You've done your best to make amends to your adult child or gatekeeper. You've taught yourself how to be more compassionate, to be patient, and to let go. You've nourished your body and mind, and you've explored spirituality.

If you're still dealing with alienation and estrangement from your family, you might be feeling discouraged, frustrated, confused, or outraged by their behavior. You understand that they need their own healing and may have unresolved anger or hurt that they are projecting onto you. But you can't fathom why this has resulted in banishment and how the crimes you may have committed deserve such extreme and harsh punishment. There is no way to know if, when, or how your child will have a change of heart. You can't control their perceptions and mind-sets, and if there were a way around, behind, under, or above all this, you would have found it by now. It's completely out of your hands.

If you have endured years of estrangement, you've learned how to be courageous, hopeful, and resilient. You've managed to keep your sanity. You've gone on with your life, accepting an unwelcome new reality. You've grown and acquired some hard-won wisdom. No doubt these years have been tougher than you could imagine. In the words of Mary Anne Radmacher, "Courage doesn't always roar. Sometimes courage is the quiet voice at the end of the day saying, 'I will try again tomorrow.'"

Not too long ago, I woke up at 3 a.m. and began ruminating and obsessing about my problems. I am aware that the brain is often overactive when we wake up in the middle of the sleep cycle, and our challenges can seem larger than life. I was feeling overwhelmed by grief and fear. After a torturous half-hour or so, I remembered to open my little mental survival tool chest and take out the appropriate tools. For example, I took some deep, slow breaths. With each negative thought, I created a positive turnaround thought. I reminded myself that I was experiencing "night talk" and that I would feel better in the morning. Unfortunately, in this case, I couldn't get back to sleep, so by morning, I felt even worse. Again, I applied techniques I have discovered along the way, like making a good, strong cup of coffee (which helped), eating a healthy breakfast (which also helped), and reading something inspirational (also helpful). I felt better and continued to use my special tools throughout the day, such as deliberately practicing positive thinking, staying calm, hopeful, grateful, and loving toward myself and others.

Albert Camus said, "Sometimes, carrying on, just carrying on, is the superhuman achievement." Each day, as your estrangement wears on, continue to take control of your life. The only way it will get better is if *you* get better. Be tough with yourself. Discipline yourself to grow, to learn, and to practice gratitude for what you have. Find happiness in the small things. Share what you've learned by giving back to others who may need your help.

And one day, with the grace of all that is holy, may you have a loving reunion with your adult child and grandchildren. Until then, keep your heart open and carry on.

Never cease loving a person, and never give up hope for him, for even the prodigal son who had fallen most low could still be saved.
—Søren Kierkegaard

94. Loving Them Anyway

> I am not what happened to me, I am what I choose to become.
>
> —Carl Jung

Several years ago, after describing to a friend how upset I was following a troubling encounter with my son and daughter-in-law, he said, "Love them anyway." I knew immediately that this was good advice.

It does no good to hold onto resentments. I've done my time: I've cried, ranted, faced my grief head on, worked through my issues, and forgiven myself and others. Now it's time to remember my friend's words and come from a place of love for all concerned.

Author Louise Erdrich wrote, "You have to love. You have to feel. It is the reason you are here on earth. You are here to risk your heart. You are here to be swallowed up. And when it happens that you are broken, or betrayed, or left, or hurt, or death brushes near, let yourself sit by an apple tree and listen to the apples falling all around you in heaps, wasting their sweetness. Tell yourself you tasted as many as you could."

My son is living his life with whatever tools and knowledge he's acquired so far. With each day, he grows and learns; with each breath, each heartbeat, he is evolving. Like every human being, he will trip and fall and get lost along the way. But though I am absent in his life, I believe that in his heart of hearts, he knows I am still and will forever be a part of him.

One day, I hope my son will wake up and understand how fully, how deeply I love him. He may suddenly miss me, miss my voice, my laugh. I hope he will want to heal and reconcile. I also hope that he will come to understand that I never left him and never stopped loving him. Every day, I send him my love and say, in my heart, "Be well, my son, be well."

So let us bless our children and grandchildren. Let us send them love, keep our hearts open, and remember the beautiful, deep connection we will always have with them.

Let love be our legacy.

Epilogue

There are no specific methods that are guaranteed to ease the heaviness in our hearts. It is a day-to-day quest for effective ways to take care of ourselves, grow in consciousness, and move forward. It can be daunting, but every now and then, we may stop for a moment and realize that the work we've been doing is beginning to bear fruit. We've learned how to successfully cope and, at times, even enjoy life. We've learned that accepting reality won't kill us, but by doing so, we invite a certain peace. We can take deep breaths again and rest in the soundless space between our thoughts. We can take great pleasure in sharing a meal with friends or taking an evening stroll under the stars. We experience a childlike wonder watching the movement of clouds as they cast shadows upon the earth.

We go on, because we choose to and need to. In doing so, we reach beyond our habitual ruminating and discover a more authentic way of being. We feel reverence for the ephemeral nature of everything, the beauty of a fleeting moment and the inevitability of transformation. And we learn the importance of detachment, because it offers a higher perspective, lifting us up from the prison of our circumstances.

If we are separated from our adult child and grandchildren at this time, it's tempting to stay stuck in a state of mind that propagates resentment, guilt, grief, and depression. But these feelings only energize pain and negativity. We've been there already. We have wept cleansing tears. We have been through hell and survived the flames of anguish. The miracle is that our brave and loving hearts still beat within our chests.

We've come a long way.

Know that our lives have meaning and value. Know that happiness comes from within, from our spirit, and can never come from anyone or anything outside of us. Let us lift up our voices and be heard. Let us search for our true home, our holy ground, and find refuge in our own perfect, loving being.

> May we have peace.
> May we have peace that is unshakable.
> May we have peace that surpasses understanding.
> May we have peace that is born of enlightenment,
> grace, and love.
> May we have peace from knowing that with every breath,
> with every beat of our hearts,
> we are healing
> just a little more.

About the Author

Nancy Lee Klune holds a master's degree in music with continuing graduate studies in counseling psychology. She has worked as a teacher, music therapist, and activities director in the field of addiction. A former professional dancer/choreographer, she is also a classical pianist, composer, and the author of several children's books. She currently coaches people dealing with alienation and estrangement. Visit her online at www.grandparentsdeniedaccess.com.

Made in the USA
Coppell, TX
12 October 2022